KU-741-881

simple ways to success

italian

Ursula Ferrigno

photography by Peter Cassidy

First published exclusively for J Sainsbury plc in 2003 by Quadrille Publishing Limited
Alhambra House 27-31, Charing Cross Road, London WC2H OLS

Editorial director Jane O'Shea **Creative director** Helen Lewis
Managing editor Janet Illsley **Art direction and design** Vanessa Courtier
Photographer Peter Cassidy **Food stylist** Linda Tubby **Props stylist** Jane Campsie
Editor Susan Fleming **Production** Vincent Smith and Jane Rogers

Text © 2003 Ursula Ferrigno Photography © 2003 Peter Cassidy
Design and layout © 2003 Quadrille Publishing Limited

The right of Ursula Ferrigno to be identified as Author of this Work has been asserted by her in
accordance with the Copyright, Designs and Patents Act 1988.
All rights reserved. No part of this book may be reproduced, stored in a retrieval system or
transmitted in any form or by any means, electronic, electrostatic, magnetic tape, mechanical,
photocopying, recording or otherwise, without the prior permission in writing of the publisher.

Cataloguing in Publication Data: a catalogue record for this book is available from the British Library.

ISBN 1 84400 051 6
Printed in China

contents

Notes

All spoon measures are level unless otherwise stated:
1 teaspoon = 5 ml spoon; 1 tablespoon = 15 ml spoon.

Use fresh herbs unless dried herbs are suggested.

Use sea salt and freshly ground black pepper unless otherwise stated.

Free-range eggs are recommended and large eggs should be used
except where a different size is specified.

Recipes which feature raw or lightly cooked eggs should be avoided
by anyone who is pregnant or in a vulnerable health group.

introduction

Italian cuisine is arguably the most delectable, the most influential, in short, the best loved cuisine in the world. Italian recipes have made an enormous difference to the way we cook. Quite apart from the perpetual presence of the best known Italian exports in our lives – pasta, pizza and Parmesan cheese, to name a few – so many things we eat have their roots in Italian cuisine. The way we assemble a salad, prepare a pasta dish, or grill a piece of fish or meat, indicate how strong these influences are. When the preparation of food is at its simplest and best, more often than not it owes a debt to the Italian kitchen.

That Italian cooking is so simple, virtually guarantees success every time you start to work in the kitchen. I truly believe that the essence of good food lies in its simplicity, and endorse the popular Italian saying '*piu se spenne peggio se magna*' (the more you spend the less well you eat). Italian food is not expensive or difficult: it's all about good basic ingredients, simply prepared and lovingly cooked, to produce a totally memorable meal that hasn't taken all day to create. When you come home from work tired and hungry, there is nothing simpler than a bruschetta with an interesting topping (possibly one that is already in the storecupboard), or a plate of pasta served with a fast sauce (see pages 86–7).

There are no difficult techniques to master in Italian cooking, although pasta-making and bread-making are more time-consuming and a little more complex. Both lie at the heart of the Italian eating experience and once you have learnt the simple rules, you will be able to create fabulous breads, pizzas and homemade pasta. I love making breads, and think of the live dough in its bowl as a friend in the kitchen, something that is growing, something to be nurtured, until it is ready to be made into a delectable bread, or indeed pizza. Because Italian cooking is essentially easy, it inspires confidence in the kitchen. And a confident cook, working with good ingredients, is a successful cook.

All the recipes here are easily achievable. All are authentically Italian, and even those I've invented myself have their roots firmly in Italian tradition. Having been brought up in Italy, and having learned the huge respect accorded to food and eating at first hand, my recipes could be nothing other than traditional. The book is roughly arranged as an Italian meal would be, beginning with easy antipasti or starters, soups and breads. The course that follows – pasta, polenta or risotto – is also simple. Neither of these courses needs to be large in volume, because there are still three more to follow – meat or seafood, vegetables and dessert. But if this meal structure sounds daunting, it need not be. Many Italians eat only a 'full meal' on special occasions, or at the weekend, when there is more time to cook – and more time to talk, argue, laugh, savour and enjoy.

Enjoyment is the most characteristic aspect of Italian cooking and eating, and I hope that the recipes here will persuade you into the kitchen, that they will enhance your life, and give you endless pleasure.

the Italian storecupboard

The essence of Italian cooking, apart from its simplicity, is its freshness, and meat or fish, vegetables and fruit are bought daily in Italy and chosen according to the season. But there are certain essentials, which will be kept in the storecupboard or *la dispensa* and renewed regularly when needed. The Italian storecupboard – indeed anyone's storecupboard – should be stocked so that the basics for a delicious meal are always at hand.

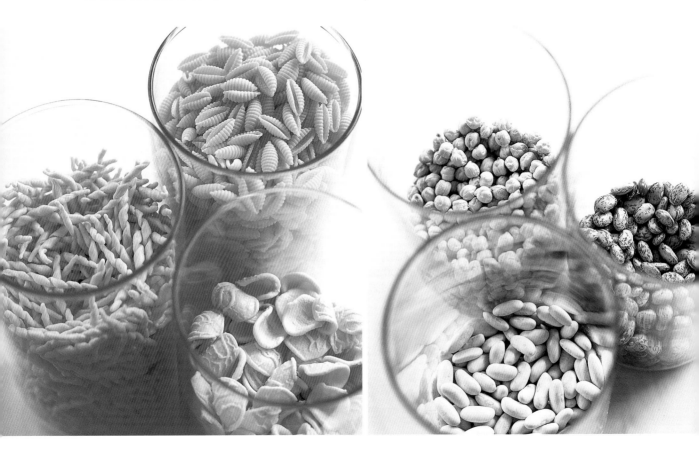

Pasta

Perhaps surprisingly, Italians tend to eat more dried pasta than fresh. Pasta is made at home, but usually only for special occasions. For the daily pasta course, the choice would normally be dried. I suggest you keep a selection of different types in your storecupboard: long pasta, such as tagliatelle and spaghetti; short pasta such as macaroni, conchiglie, farfalle and fusilli; and pastina or very small pasta shapes.

Choose the variety of pasta according to the sauce you intend to serve. Long ribbon pastas of varying thicknesses, such as tagliatelle, are best served with butter, tomato, cream and fish sauces. Spaghetti and linguine are matched by pesto, tomato, fish and meat sauces, including Bolognese of course. Short pasta shapes such as orecchiette and conchiglie, are best with vegetable sauces, the curves and indentations of the pasta ideal for holding small morsels of sauce. And the tiny shapes of pastina – from stellini to farfalline – are destined for soups.

Rice and grains

Italy relies on many grains, but the most important is wheat, which is made into flours for bread and pasta. Wheat flours come in a number of forms, graded by their fineness and suitability for different types of cooking. The best Italian storecupboard would contain farina '00' or *doppio zero* for making fresh pasta, pastry and cakes; '0' grade for pizza; and semolino duro, a ground durum wheat flour used in the making of commercial pasta and gnocchi. There would also be strong unbleached flour for bread-making, plain flour for pastry and self-raising flour for cakes. Farro is an ancient type of wheat also known as spelt. It is now enjoying a resurgence in popularity, and is being cultivated for use mainly in soups, like my farro and bean soup (page 51).

Rice, grown in the valley of the Po river and its tributaries in the north of Italy, is another staple. Risotto is the most famous of Italy's rice dishes and there are three main varieties of risotto rice available in this country – arborio, carnaroli and vialone nano. The principal characteristic of risotto rice is its ability to absorb moisture, thus enlarging the grain. The grain softens and develops a creamy texture, while retaining a bite, described as *al dente* (to the tooth). Rice is also used in soups, snacks, salads, stuffings and as a main course accompaniment.

The third most important grain for the storecupboard is polenta. This is made with a yellow maize or white corn flour. A staple in northern Italy, polenta is available in two forms. The one I prefer is the standard coarse grain, which needs up to 40 minutes to cook. The other is a quick-cook polenta that may not be quite as tasty, but is perfectly acceptable when enriched with butter and cheese. Polenta can be served 'wet', straight from the pan, as an accompaniment to a meat, mushroom or vegetable stew or sauce. Or it can be left until cold and set, then sliced and served instead of bread, or the slices may be fried or grilled to accompany meats, poultry or game birds, or sausages. Sometimes set polenta is enriched with butter, cheese and other flavourings.

Pulses

When in season, legumes or pulses are eaten fresh in Italy, but in this country they are most commonly found dried. With a packet of dried cannellini or borlotti beans, chick peas or Castelluccio lentils in your storecupboard, you will never be short of something to cook that will be nutritious and satisfying. Most pulses require long soaking to rehydrate them, and then take quite a time to cook. If you are short of time, however, canned pulses are a good alternative and make good standby items.

Nuts and seeds

These need to be bought fresh and used fairly regularly. Nuts and seeds, for instance, contain oils, which can turn rancid. (Storing in the fridge or freezer helps prolong their life.) Walnuts, hazelnuts, almonds and pine nuts are used extensively in Italian cooking, in both sweet and savoury dishes. Seeds, such as fennel, aniseed and sesame, make wonderful flavourings and garnishes, and they are highly nutritious.

Dried fruit

Keep a selection of ready-to-eat dried apricots, prunes, figs, raisins and sultanas in your storecupboard to use for breads, desserts and sweets. If possible, buy organic dried fruit that has not been preserved with sulphur dioxide.

Oils and butter

Olive oil is the bottled essence of Italy. It is used extensively here now, particularly since the virtues of the so-called 'Mediterranean diet' and its almost exclusive use of olive oil became known. Oils are graded according to acidity – extra virgin olive oil has the lowest acidity, is the purest and most flavourful. Thrifty housekeepers – whether from Umbria, Puglia, Tuscany or Liguria – will always have a bottle or two of the local new season's oil (available from November usually), which they will use only for dressings and as a condiment – sprinkled generously over a thick soup, for instance.

Extra virgin olive oil is best reserved for dressings. It is not used in cooking, as heat damages the proteins. Virgin olive oil is usually produced from more mature olives, is higher in acidity, and can be used for light cooking or in dressings such as mayonnaise. Straightforward olive oil is what you should use for cooking. This is also the oil to utilise for preserving vegetables or making a flavoured oil. I like to do this at Christmas time: olive oil in a nice bottle, with floating herbs, chillies and garlic, makes a good present for friends and family.

Unsalted butter is another Italian cooking medium, used mainly in the north, although it features in cake and biscuit making throughout the rest of the country.

Cheeses

The most vital cheese in the Italian storecupboard is Parmesan, as it has so many uses. It is perishable and should therefore be kept in the fridge, but it has a good shelf life. Keep a piece ready for grating, well wrapped in the salad drawer of the fridge to prevent it drying out. To use at its best, buy little and often.

Vinegars

A selection of vinegars will feature in any Italian storecupboard. Red and white wine vinegars are both used in cooking and salad dressings, but the most highly prized vinegar in Italy is balsamic or *aceto balsamico*. This is probably the most expensive condiment in the Italian kitchen, because the maturation process is so lengthy and involved, but a drop or two of an aged balsamic can transform a dish. The finest balsamic vinegars, labelled *aceto balsamico tradizionale di Modena*, are over 30 years old, but you can buy less expensive and still exceptionally good balsamic vinegar aged from 5 to 20 years (similarly labelled but missing the word *tradizionale*).

Basic flavourings

The primary flavouring spices of any kitchen, including the Italian one, are salt, pepper and sugar. I always use sea salt (coarse and flake varieties, and fine table salt), and grind my pepper freshly from black peppercorns. Of the sugars, I keep golden caster, granulated, soft brown and icing sugar. I also store a vanilla pod in a container of caster sugar, so I always have some fragrant vanilla sugar to hand.

Herbs, spices and aromatics

Most Italian housekeepers would have fresh herbs almost constantly to hand in pots on the windowsill or in the garden – basil, flat leaf parsley, marjoram, thyme, sage and mint in particular. However, dried oregano is an essential storecupboard item, and one of the few herbs which is actually improved by drying. If you have oregano in the garden, you can dry small bunches in an airing cupboard, if you like.

Dried bay leaves are also worth stocking, and you can dry these if you have a bay tree in the garden. Garlic is, of course, a vital flavouring in many Italian dishes, so you will need to keep a supply of fresh garlic bulbs.

Dried chillies are very popular in southern Italy and small, fiery red chillies, called peperoncini, appear in a variety of dishes. These are available dried, but should be used cautiously as they are very hot.

The other spices most commonly encountered are nutmeg, juniper berries, ground paprika, cinnamon, cloves and saffron. Keep whole nutmeg and grate freshly as required. Ready-ground spices should be bought and used frequently, as they lose flavour during lengthy storage. Saffron is best bought as threads as these are less liable to be adulterated than the powdered alternative. This revered and expensive spice is used for a classic risotto milanese. Vanilla pods and vanilla extract lend an inimitable flavour to many Italian desserts and ice creams.

Dried mushrooms
These are a primary source of flavour in the Italian kitchen and a packet or two of dried porcini or ceps is essential in the storecupboard. Fresh wild mushrooms are collected and eaten enthusiastically all over Italy in the autumn, but at other times of year, they are used dried – and lend extraordinary flavour to many dishes. Rehydrate by soaking in warm water to cover for about 20 minutes (strain and save the water for stock, as it will be full of flavour).

Other storecupboard essentials

There are so many important storecupboard items in an Italian kitchen, it is hard to name them all. The tomato, which is essential in so many Italian dishes, will be on the shelves in various guises. Canned plum tomatoes, whole or chopped (often with added herbs), sit alongside passata (cooked puréed tomatoes), sun-dried tomatoes and, perhaps, sun-dried tomato paste.

Artichokes are preserved in oil, capers are brined or salted, and anchovies are salted or preserved in oil. (The salt from capers and anchovies must be rinsed off before use.) Olives are preserved in brine or oil, often with other flavourings; my favourite is the Gaeta olive. Truffles flavour oils or are condensed with ceps to make an expensive, but delicious, paste. A can or two of tuna, in brine or oil, can be used in a matter of moments to make a salad or sauce.

On the sweet side, I like to have jars of apricot jam and honey available – good on breakfast toast, or in baking and desserts. I'm not a chocoholic, but some good dark chocolate is great in puddings, as is cocoa powder. Even the coffee beans so vital for the espresso, can be used in cooking. And I always keep amaretti biscuits, to serve with coffee, use in my dessert recipes, or crumble over ice cream.

The Italian storecupboard should also boast a limited selection of alcohol. Red and white wines, vermouth, Marsala and Vin Santo, and spirits such as brandy and the uniquely Italian grappa, add flavour and character to many sauces and desserts.

1 antipasti

warm seafood salad

Insalata calla di mare is a very popular antipasto, and every region of Italy has its own version. You can vary the fish, but do include a variety of textures, avoiding oily fish, as the flavour would be too pronounced. This salad is best served warm.

SERVES 6

500g (1lb 2oz) fresh mussels
2 tablespoons dry white wine
1 dried chilli
500g (1lb 2oz) squid, cleaned
2 tablespoons white wine vinegar
1 onion, peeled and halved
2 bay leaves
500g (1lb 2oz) monkfish fillet, skinned

6 scallops, shelled and cleaned
12 large raw prawns in shell
sea salt and freshly ground black pepper
handful of black olives, to serve

FOR THE DRESSING:

1 garlic clove, peeled and crushed
handful of flat leaf parsley, finely chopped
3 tablespoons lemon juice
3 tablespoons virgin olive oil

1   Discard any broken mussels, and those that do not close when sharply tapped. Scrub the mussels thoroughly in cold water and pull out the beards, then place in a large saucepan with the wine. Cover and cook over a high heat for about 4 minutes until they open, shaking the pan occasionally. Lift out the mussels with a slotted spoon, discarding any that remain closed. When cool enough to handle, shell the mussels and place in a bowl. Pour the cooking liquor through a muslin-lined strainer on to the mussels. Add the dried chilli, stir and set aside.

2   Rinse the squid well and cut the pouches into 1cm (½ inch) rings, keeping the tentacles whole (if available). Put 1.5 litres (2½ pints) water into a saucepan with 1 tablespoon of the vinegar, the onion, 1 bay leaf and some salt, and bring to the boil. Add the squid and cook at a steady simmer until opaque and you can pierce them with a fork, about 5 minutes depending on size. Remove with a slotted spoon, drain well and add to the mussels.

3   Cut the monkfish into large chunks and add to the water in which the squid was cooked. Simmer gently for about 2 minutes. Remove from the heat, leaving the fish in the liquid.

4   Meanwhile, heat 300ml (½ pint) water in another pan with the remaining bay leaf and vinegar, and some salt. When it comes to the boil, add the scallops and simmer gently for 2 minutes. Remove with a slotted spoon and set aside with the mussels and squid. Add the prawns to the scallop cooking water, bring to a simmer and cook for 1 minute. Drain and, when cool enough to handle, peel, leaving the tail shell on if you like. Drain the monkfish and add to the other seafood with the prawns. Remove and discard the chilli.

5   For the dressing, combine the garlic, parsley and lemon juice in a small bowl. Add a generous grind of black pepper and some salt. Whisk in the olive oil, then taste and adjust the seasoning. Toss the seafood with the dressing and divide between shallow bowls. Serve immediately, while still warm, scattered with the olives.

stuffed mussels

A really tasty classic from Campania, the region where I was brought up, which can be served with a wedge of lemon for a simple antipasto. The mussels are cooked to open, then topped in their half shell with a stuffing of garlic, parsley and breadcrumbs and baked briefly. The stuffing is a basic recipe to which other ingredients, such as tomato sauce and capers, can be added.

SERVES 4

1kg (2¼lb) mussels
2 unwaxed lemons, cut into quarters
4 garlic cloves, peeled
3 tablespoons dry white wine
4 tablespoons olive oil
large handful of flat leaf parsley, finely
  chopped
125g (4oz) fresh white breadcrumbs
  (slightly dry)
sea salt and freshly ground black pepper
lemon wedges, to serve

1 Preheat the oven to 220°C (fan oven 200°C), gas mark 7. Discard any broken mussels, and those that do not close when sharply tapped. Scrub the mussels thoroughly in cold water and pull out the little beards.

2 Put the lemon quarters, garlic and white wine into a large sauté pan or wide saucepan. Add the mussels, cover with a tight-fitting lid and cook over a high heat for 5 minutes until the shells open, shaking the pan occasionally. Discard any mussels that remain closed.

3 Using a slotted spoon, remove the mussels from the pan, reserving the liquor. Remove and discard the empty half shells. Loosen the mussels in the bottom shells and place the shells on a baking sheet.

4 Filter the reserved cooking liquor through a muslin-lined strainer into a bowl. Mix in the olive oil, parsley, breadcrumbs and salt and pepper to taste.

5 Spoon a little of the parsley and breadcrumb mixture over each mussel. Bake in the oven for about 7 minutes until the topping is golden brown. Serve hot, with lemon wedges.

bruschetta

Originating from Rome, bruschetta are slices of coarse country bread, baked until crisp and slightly charred, then rubbed with garlic and drizzled with olive oil. For centuries, bruschetta has been a staple of the poor, usually eaten to celebrate the new season's olive oil. Nowadays it is typically served as an appetiser, while you wait for your pasta to be ready. Bruschetta is also excellent with fish soups, and pan-fried chicken livers. I like to use Pugliese bread.

MAKES 6

6 slices of coarse white Italian bread, about 3cm (1¼ inches) thick
2 garlic cloves, peeled and halved

about 6 tablespoons extra virgin olive oil, to drizzle
sea salt and freshly ground black pepper

1 Preheat the grill or a griddle pan and heat the oven to 220°C (fan oven 200°C), gas mark 7. Score the bread slices lightly with the point of a small knife in a criss-cross fashion, then grill or griddle to toast on both sides.

2 While still hot, rub the toasted surface all over with the cut garlic cloves. Put the toast slices on a baking sheet and bake in the oven for 2 minutes to crisp them through.

3 Drizzle about 1 tablespoon extra virgin oil over each slice. Sprinkle generously with pepper and a little salt, then serve.

broad bean purée

A wonderful purée to be enjoyed during the all too brief, early summer broad bean season. You can spread it on crostini moistened with olive oil, or serve the purée piled up in a dish surrounded by crostini. It is also delicious spread on bruschetta (page 21), wonderful in a panino with some pecorino cheese, and it can be served as a dip with crudités. One of my favourite restaurants serves a broad bean purée topped with grilled scallops and roasted cherry tomatoes. When fresh broad beans are unavailable, make the purée with frozen beans.

Illustrated on previous page

SERVES 6–8
500g (1lb 2oz) podded fresh or frozen
  broad beans
2 garlic cloves, peeled
50g (2oz) crustless white bread
about 2 tablespoons milk
5 tablespoons extra virgin olive oil
sea salt and freshly ground black pepper
FOR THE CROSTINI:
12–16 slices of ciabatta bread
extra virgin olive oil, to drizzle

1 Cook the fresh or frozen beans in a saucepan of simmering water, to which you have added 1 garlic clove, at a low simmer for about 5 minutes. When the beans are tender, drain them and the garlic, reserving 2 tablespoons of the liquid. Set aside to cool.

2 Place the bread in a bowl and pour on enough milk to moisten it. Slip the broad beans out of their white skins and discard the skins. This will give you a really creamy purée.

3 Put the bright emerald beans, both garlic cloves and the bread with its milk into a food processor. Whiz to a purée, gradually adding the olive oil through the funnel. If the purée is very thick, add a little of the reserved bean cooking liquid. Taste and adjust the seasoning.

4 For the crostini, preheat the oven to 180°C (fan oven 160°C), gas mark 4. Bake the ciabatta slices in the oven until crisp and golden, about 10–12 minutes. Moisten the crostini with a little extra virgin olive oil, then serve with the broad bean purée.

chicken liver crostini

In Tuscany where this dish comes from, the robust chicken liver, garlic and wine mixture is served on baked ciabatta crostini. If you prefer, you can use bruschetta (page 21) instead, allowing one per person. It's a familiar concept throughout Europe, each country having its own variation.

SERVES 6–8

250g (9oz) chicken livers
2 tablespoons olive oil
1 celery stalk, finely chopped
1 shallot, peeled and very finely chopped
2 small garlic cloves, peeled and chopped
generous handful of flat leaf parsley, chopped
125g (4oz) lean beef mince
1 tablespoon tomato purée

6 tablespoons dry white wine
12–16 slices of ciabatta bread
1 tablespoon capers, rinsed and chopped
2 salted anchovy fillets, rinsed and finely chopped
100g (3½oz) unsalted butter
extra virgin olive oil, to drizzle
sea salt and freshly ground black pepper

1 Trim the fat and gristle from the chicken livers, then rinse, pat dry with kitchen paper and chop finely. Set aside.

2 Heat the olive oil in a saucepan and, when just hot, add the celery, shallot, garlic and parsley. Cook for about 10 minutes until soft, stirring frequently.

3 Add the chicken livers and minced beef and cook over a very low heat until the livers have lost their raw colour and become crumbly. Mix in the tomato purée and cook for 1 minute.

4 Increase the heat, pour in the wine and boil to reduce until nearly all of it has evaporated. Lower the heat, and add a little salt and plenty of pepper. Simmer for 30 minutes, adding a little hot water if the mixture becomes too dry.

5 Meanwhile, preheat the oven to 180°C (fan oven 160°C), gas mark 4. For the crostini, bake the ciabatta slices until crisp and golden, about 10–12 minutes.

6 Add the capers and anchovies to the chicken liver mixture. Mix in the butter and cook gently for 5 minutes, stirring constantly. Moisten the crostini with a little extra virgin olive oil, then spread with the chicken liver mixture. Serve at once.

simple antipasti

Italians often start their main meal of the day with antipasti – tasty, light morsels that stimulate the palate for the courses to follow. Salamis, prosciutto and other cold meats are often a feature of antipasti, and seafood dishes are especially popular in coastal areas. Colourful vegetables and salads in sharp dressings bring the tastebuds to anticipatory life, too.

Antipasto has always been one of the most exciting courses for me, as I love the variety of flavours and textures on offer. And I'm delighted to see the increasing range of imported Italian antipasto foods now available in supermarkets – preserved and dried vegetables, tasty spreads and dips, interesting fresh breads, grissini (breadsticks), cured meats, cheeses, olives, capers and salted anchovies. With these you can create appetising antipasti with the minimum of time and effort. Try the following simple ideas.

▲ **prosciutto with fresh figs and mozzarella**
Drape 2 slices of prosciutto on each serving plate and top with a fresh fig half. Tear some fresh buffalo mozzarella into pieces and place alongside. Dress with a little aged balsamic vinegar and extra virgin olive oil, then sprinkle with a small handful of toasted pine nuts. Season with salt and a generous grind of black pepper, then serve, with grissini and olives.

aubergine and olives on rocket with Parmesan

Serve 3 ready-prepared preserved char-grilled aubergines, or freshly grilled oiled aubergine slices per person. Arrange on a bed of wild rocket leaves. Top each aubergine slice with 2 chopped sun-dried tomatoes in oil, a couple of anchovies (rinsed if salted), and some pitted black or green olives. Scatter over some Parmesan cheese shavings, and serve.

roasted pepper and tuna salad

To serve 4–6, roast 2 red and 2 yellow peppers at 200°C, gas 6 for 20 minutes; cool. Skin, core, deseed and chop the peppers and 6 plum tomatoes. Tear ½ ciabatta loaf into cubes, put into a bowl and moisten with 4 tbsp extra virgin olive oil. Add the peppers, tomatoes and a drained, flaked 400g can tuna in spring water. Add 2 tbsp each chopped parsley, basil and capers, and 12 pitted black olives. Drizzle with another 4 tbsp oil and 2 tbsp red wine vinegar, season well, toss and serve.

▲ artichoke, chick pea and baby spinach salad

To serve 4–6, drain and rinse a 400g can of chick peas. Drain a 280g jar of artichokes in oil and quarter the artichokes. Combine the chick peas and artichokes in a bowl with 1 finely chopped red onion. Add 2 good handfuls of baby spinach leaves, and a handful of pitted black olives. For the dressing, whisk the juice of 1 lemon with salt, pepper and 6 tbsp extra virgin olive oil. Add to the salad and toss to mix. (Tear a little mozzarella over the salad to serve if you like.)

tomatoes stuffed with breadcrumbs and parsley

Flavourful, ripe tomatoes are essential for this classical Roman antipasto dish, *pomodori ammollicati*. Make it in advance if you like, to allow time for the flavours to combine and intensify. Serve hot, warm or cold, but not chilled.

SERVES 4

6 large, ripe but firm, tomatoes (preferably
  with stalks)
olive oil, to brush
handful of flat leaf parsley, chopped
2 garlic cloves, peeled and chopped
1 tablespoon capers, rinsed and chopped
1/2 small dried hot chilli, crumbled

100g (3½oz) fresh white breadcrumbs
  (slightly dry)
1 teaspoon dried oregano
1 tablespoon extra virgin olive oil, plus extra
  to drizzle
sea salt and freshly ground black pepper
freshly grated Parmesan cheese, to serve
  (optional)

1 Cut the tops off the tomatoes and reserve. Scoop out the core and seeds, then sprinkle the cavities with salt. Lay the tomatoes, cut-side down, on kitchen paper and leave to drain for about 30 minutes.

2 Preheat the oven to 190°C (fan oven 170°C), gas mark 5. Brush the base of a shallow baking dish or roasting tin with a little olive oil. Wipe the inside of the tomatoes with kitchen paper.

3 Combine the parsley, garlic, capers, chilli, breadcrumbs and oregano in a bowl. Mix well, then stir in the extra virgin olive oil. Season with salt and pepper to taste.

4 Stand the tomatoes, cut-side up, in the prepared dish and spoon in the stuffing. Replace the tomato lids and bake in the oven for about 20 minutes until the tomatoes are soft but still whole.

5 If liked, lift the tomato lids, drizzle a little olive oil over the stuffing and sprinkle lightly with grated Parmesan. Serve hot, warm or at room temperature.

Sicilian baked aubergines

I love aubergines, and this dish is one of my favourites. The aubergine flesh is scooped out of the skins and mixed with a spicy sausagemeat and two favoured Sicilian ingredients – pine nuts and currants. This mixture is piled back into the aubergine skins, then baked in the oven.

SERVES 4

2 medium aubergines

4 tablespoons olive oil, plus extra to drizzle

1 large garlic clove, peeled and crushed

2 shallots, peeled and finely chopped

1 celery stalk, chopped

250g (9oz) spicy pork sausage, skinned

125g (4oz) fresh white breadcrumbs

2 tablespoons pine nuts

2 tablespoons capers, rinsed and dried

1 egg, beaten

2 teaspoons dried oregano

2 tablespoons freshly grated Parmesan cheese

1 tablespoon currants

1 large ripe tomato, cut into strips

sea salt and freshly ground black pepper

1 Cut the aubergines in half lengthways. Scoop out the flesh, using a small sharp knife and then a small teaspoon, leaving a thin layer inside the skin. Be careful not to pierce the skin.

2 Chop the aubergine pulp coarsely and place in a colander. Sprinkle with salt, mix well and set aside to drain for 20 minutes.

3 Heat 3 tablespoons of the olive oil in a frying pan. Add the garlic, shallots and celery, and sauté over a low heat until soft, stirring frequently. Add the sausagemeat, in small pieces, and cook for 20 minutes, turning frequently.

4 Meanwhile, preheat the oven to 180°C (fan oven 160°C), gas mark 4. Squeeze the liquid from the aubergine pulp, rinse to remove excess salt, drain and pat dry with kitchen paper. Add the aubergine pulp to the pan and fry gently, stirring, for a few minutes. Taste and adjust the seasoning.

5 Add the breadcrumbs to the frying pan and cook, stirring, for 2–3 minutes. Stir in the pine nuts and cook for a further 30 seconds, then transfer to a bowl. Add the capers, egg, oregano, Parmesan, currants and salt and pepper. Mix thoroughly, taste and adjust the seasoning.

6 Oil a deep baking dish with the remaining 1 tablespoon olive oil. Pat the inside of the aubergine shells dry, then place side by side in the dish and fill with the sausage mixture. Lay the tomato strips on the top and drizzle with a little olive oil. Pour 150ml (¼ pint) water into the bottom of the dish. Cover with foil and bake for 20 minutes, then remove the foil and bake for a further 20 minutes. Serve the dish warm, an hour after you take it from the oven.

braised shallots

Braised in wine with grapes, these shallots often form part of a spectacular Piedmontese antipasto, served either hot or cold. They may also accompany cold meats, or you can serve them hot with braised meat dishes. In Italy, white, squat onions called *borratine* are used. These are hard to find in this country, so I always use shallots.

SERVES 4

750g (1lb 10oz) shallots
3 tablespoons olive oil
25g (1oz) unsalted butter
2 teaspoons tomato purée
1 tablespoon caster sugar
2 tablespoons red wine vinegar
250g (9oz) seedless black grapes
sea salt and freshly ground black pepper

1 Add the shallots to a pan of boiling water, bring back to the boil and blanch for 1 minute. Drain and remove the skins and root ends, taking care to keep the root base intact, as this holds the shallot together during cooking.

2 Heat the olive oil and butter in a large sauté pan. Add the shallots and sauté for about 12 minutes until golden, shaking the pan frequently.

3 Dissolve the tomato purée in 2 teaspoons of hot water and add to the pan with the sugar, vinegar, grapes and salt and pepper. Cook, uncovered, for about 25 minutes until the shallots are tender and a nice brown colour, adding a little water if necessary. Serve the shallots hot or cold, but not chilled.

stuffed mushrooms

A wonderful combination of intense flavours – anchovy, nutmeg, garlic and marjoram – is piled into big field mushrooms and baked to serve as an antipasto. It's a very light and tasty first course, which can also be served as a side dish to meat. Try using other mushrooms, such as large chestnut mushrooms.

SERVES 4

50g (2oz) dried porcini mushrooms
4 large mushrooms
2 anchovy fillets in oil, drained
1 garlic clove, peeled
handful of marjoram leaves

100g (3½oz) fresh white breadcrumbs
pinch of freshly grated nutmeg
2 tablespoons olive oil, plus extra to drizzle
handful of flat leaf parsley, finely chopped
sea salt and freshly ground black pepper

1 Soak the dried porcini in warm water to cover for 10 minutes. Drain and pat dry with kitchen paper. (Save the soaking water to use as stock for another dish if you like.)

2 Preheat the oven to 200°C (fan oven 180°C), gas mark 6. Gently wipe the fresh mushrooms with damp kitchen paper to clean them. Detach the stems and reserve.

3 Chop the soaked porcini, mushroom stems, anchovies, garlic and marjoram together. Tip into a bowl and add the breadcrumbs, nutmeg and salt and pepper to taste. Mix thoroughly.

4 Heat the olive oil in a frying pan over a medium heat. Add the mushroom and breadcrumb mixture and sauté for 5 minutes.

5 Lay the mushroom caps on an oiled baking sheet, hollow-side up. Season lightly with salt and then fill them with the crumb mixture. Sprinkle parsley on top of each stuffed mushroom and drizzle with a little olive oil. Bake for about 10–15 minutes until soft. Serve at room temperature.

duck breasts with balsamic vinegar

Duck is very popular in Italy, particularly around the Puccini lake near Lucca, where the locals shoot a lot of wild duck. There is a resurgence in the popularity of farmed duck too, because of its fine flavour. It's particularly delicious dressed with balsamic vinegar and served on a bed of crisp rocket leaves, or my favourite char-grilled radicchio.

SERVES 6

2 duck breasts, each about 400g (14oz)

3 heads of radicchio

3 tablespoons aged balsamic vinegar, or a little
  more to taste

sea salt and freshly ground black pepper

1 Cut the duck breasts in half widthways. Score the skin with the tip of a small sharp knife, then rub with salt and pepper.

2 Heat a heavy-based frying pan. Place the duck breasts in the pan, skin-side down, and cook over a medium heat for about 9 minutes, depending on thickness. Pour most of the rendered fat from the pan. (Save it for sautéeing potatoes if you like.)

3 Meanwhile, preheat the grill. Quarter the radicchio and place on a lightly oiled baking tray. Grill for 7–10 minutes, turning occasionally, until slightly charred all over.

4 Spoon 1 tablespoon balsamic vinegar over the duck breasts, then turn and cook for 2 minutes on the other side. Lift out the duck breasts on to a board, cover with foil and set aside in a warm place to rest for 10 minutes.

5 In the meantime, add the remaining balsamic vinegar and 3 tablespoons warm water to the frying pan and stir well to deglaze, scraping up the sediment from the bottom of the pan. Taste for seasoning and add a little more balsamic vinegar if required.

6 Carve the duck crossways into 1cm (½ inch) slices and arrange on warm plates, with the char-grilled radicchio alongside. Drizzle the balsamic pan juices over the duck breast slices and serve.

mozzarella fritters with roasted cherry tomatoes

For these intensely flavoured cheesy bites, grated mozzarella and Parmesan are tossed with flour, bound with beaten egg, then fried and served with roasted cherry tomatoes on the vine. The mozzarella must be removed from its pack, drained and refrigerated for 24 hours before grating, to allow it to dry out a little. The fritters are highly popular with children.

SERVES 4

250g (9oz) mozzarella cheese, drained and dried
  slightly (see above)
125g (4oz) Parmesan cheese, freshly grated
2 tablespoons Italian '00' flour
1 large egg, lightly beaten
generous handful of basil leaves, torn
1 garlic clove, peeled and crushed
4 tablespoons olive oil
sea salt and freshly ground black pepper
FOR THE ROASTED CHERRY TOMATOES:
250g (9oz) cherry tomatoes, on the vine
olive oil, to drizzle

1 Preheat the oven to 180°C (fan oven 160°C), gas mark 4. Shred the mozzarella, using a coarse cheese grater, and place in a bowl. Add the Parmesan and flour and toss to mix, then add the beaten egg to bind, mixing thoroughly.

2 Add the torn basil, garlic and some salt and pepper, and mix well. With damp hands, shape the mixture into balls, the size of a walnut. Place on a tray and chill in the fridge for 30 minutes.

3 Place the cherry tomatoes (still on the vine) on an oiled baking tray, drizzle with a little olive oil and roast in the oven for 20 minutes until the skins split.

4 Meanwhile, heat the 4 tablespoons olive oil in a large frying pan. Fry the mozzarella fritters in batches, for about 10 minutes, turning until golden all over. Remove with a slotted spoon and drain on kitchen paper. Keep warm while you cook the rest.

5 Drizzle the roasted cherry tomatoes with a little more olive oil and season well. Serve the fritters hot, with the roasted tomatoes.

Piedmontese fondue

Fontina, the best known cheese from the Valle d'Aosta in northern Italy was originally made at Monte Fontina, hence the name. It is the main ingredient of a classic *fonduta piemontese*. The other characteristic ingredient is the white truffle of Alba. Fresh white truffle is prohibitively expensive, but you can buy truffle paste made with white truffles and porcini, which works very well in a *fonduta*. Crostini are served for dipping into the *fonduta*. Alternatively, you can use cubes of slightly dry coarse-textured bread, or thick slices of polenta (page 96).

SERVES 4
400g (14 oz) Italian fontina cheese
275ml (9 fl oz) whole milk
125g (4 oz) unsalted butter
4 egg yolks
freshly ground black pepper
1 tablespoon truffle paste (optional)
FOR THE CROSTINI:
12–16 slices of ciabatta bread

1 About 4 hours ahead of serving, cut the fontina into small dice. Place in a bowl, add enough of the milk to cover the cheese and set aside.

2 Preheat the oven to 180°C (fan oven 160°C), gas mark 4. Put the butter into a large heatproof bowl over a pan of simmering water, and add the fontina and all of the milk. Cook, stirring constantly, until the cheese has melted, about 10 minutes.

3 Meanwhile, for the crostini, bake the ciabatta slices until crisp and golden, about 10–12 minutes.

4 Beat the egg yolks into the smooth cheese mixture, one at a time. Continue to cook over the pan of simmering water, beating constantly, until the *fonduta* is the consistency of thick cream. Season with a generous grind of black pepper and remove from the heat. If you happen to be adding truffle paste, stir it in at this point.

5 Transfer the *fonduta* to warm individual bowls and serve the crostini to accompany.

2 soups

minestrone

This 'soup of the kitchen' or *minestrone della cucina*, is one born out of necessity, and the ingredients are determined by the contents of the *dispensa*, or larder. This one includes carrots, peas, celery, onion, vermouth, spaghetti broken into small pieces, and plenty of fresh parsley, but you can use whatever vegetables are around in the kitchen. A few strands of spaghetti are vital. Serve with bruschetta (page 21).

SERVES 6

1.5 litres (2½ pints) chicken broth (page 47)
2 tablespoons olive oil
1 onion, peeled and finely chopped
3 bay leaves
2 garlic cloves, peeled and chopped
handful of flat leaf parsley, chopped
2 celery stalks, trimmed and sliced
2 large carrots, peeled and roughly chopped
1 parsnip, peeled and roughly chopped
2 leeks, washed, trimmed and finely sliced
200g (7oz) podded fresh or frozen peas
  (preferably fresh)
12 strands of spaghetti, broken into
  short lengths
2 tablespoons sweet vermouth
sea salt and freshly ground black pepper

1 Pour the chicken broth into a large saucepan and bring to a simmer.

2 Heat the olive oil in another large saucepan, add the onion and sauté gently for about 5 minutes until golden. Add the bay leaves, garlic and parsley and stir. Add the celery, carrots, parsnip and leeks, and sauté until slightly softened.

3 Add the warmed chicken broth to the pan and bring to the boil. Add the peas, pasta and vermouth, and simmer for 20 minutes until the vegetables are all tender. Taste for seasoning, then serve, in warm bowls with country style bread.

lettuce in broth

Stuffed vegetables are a source of pride in the cooking of Liguria. Here lettuce leaves are stuffed with dried porcini, Parmesan, fresh marjoram and breadcrumbs, then cooked in a fine broth.

SERVES 6

25g (1oz) dried porcini mushrooms

125g (4oz) coarse, fresh white breadcrumbs
   (slightly dry)

3 tablespoons milk

6 Little Gem lettuces

2 garlic cloves, peeled and chopped

2 tablespoons chopped marjoram leaves

2 eggs, beaten

25g (1oz) Parmesan cheese, freshly grated

1 egg white, beaten

6 or 12 slices of firm, coarse-textured bread

6 tablespoons extra virgin olive oil

1.5 litres (2½ pints) chicken or vegetable
   broth (page 47)

sea salt and freshly ground black pepper

1 Preheat the oven to 180°C (fan oven 160°C), gas mark 4. Soak the dried porcini in warm water for 10 minutes, then drain and chop. Soak the breadcrumbs in the milk for 5 minutes, then squeeze dry. Discard the outermost leaves from the lettuces, then carefully extract the hearts, keeping the heads intact.

2 Chop two of the lettuce hearts and place in a bowl (save the rest for a salad). Add the porcini, garlic, breadcrumbs and marjoram. Mix in the eggs, Parmesan and seasoning.

3 Blanch the lettuce heads in a pan of boiling water for a few seconds. Drain, open carefully and fill with the prepared stuffing. Re-close, brushing with the beaten egg white to seal and hold in the filling.

4 Brush the bread slices liberally with 5 tablespoons olive oil, place on a baking sheet and toast in the oven for about 10 minutes. Meanwhile, heat the remaining olive oil and 4 tablespoons of the broth in a wide saucepan, add the stuffed lettuces and cook, covered, for a few minutes over a low heat, turning occasionally. Bring the rest of the broth to the boil in another pan. Put one or two toast slices into each warm soup bowl, add a stuffed lettuce and pour the hot broth over to serve.

Tuscan leek and tomato soup

This is a variant on the classic Tuscan *pappa con pomodoro*, a simple soup, made here with fresh tomatoes, leeks, the best possible broth, and the finest extra virgin olive oil. The inclusion of bread is typically Italian – even when stale, bread is never wasted and it adds texture to a soup.

SERVES 6

8 young leeks, trimmed
50ml (2 fl oz) olive oil
675g (1 1/2 lb) ripe tomatoes
1/2 teaspoon dried red chilli flakes
250g (9 oz) crusty day-old bread
750ml (1 1/4 pints) chicken or vegetable broth
  (page 47)
6 basil leaves
extra virgin olive oil, to drizzle
sea salt and freshly ground black pepper

1 Wash the leeks well under cold running water. Drain, then chop finely. Heat the olive oil in a large saucepan, add the leeks and fry gently for 10 minutes.

2 Meanwhile, whiz the tomatoes in a blender or food processor to a purée (then sieve to remove skins and seeds if you prefer, though this isn't essential). Add to the leeks with the chilli and some salt and pepper. Bring to the boil and simmer for 20 minutes.

3 Break the bread into small pieces and add to the pan. Stir well and simmer gently for 5 minutes. Pour in the broth, mix well and simmer for a further 10 minutes.

4 Pour the soup into warm bowls and add a basil leaf to each serving. Drizzle with a little extra virgin olive oil and serve.

la ribollita

A thick Tuscan soup made with good day-old bread, assorted vegetables and fresh (or dried) beans. It is traditionally made one day ahead, hence the name *ribollita*, which means 'he-boiled'. The vegetables here are only a suggestion, as you can use any combination, so long as you have the basic *soffritto* flavouring of onion, celery and carrot. For instance, you could substitute Savoy cabbage for the cavolo nero, and use a 400g can of cannellini beans instead of the dried beans.

SERVES 6

175g (6oz) dried cannellini beans, soaked in
  cold water overnight
4 tablespoons olive oil
1 large onion, peeled and finely sliced
4 carrots, peeled and chopped
4 celery stalks, chopped
4 leeks, washed, trimmed and chopped
2 garlic cloves, peeled and crushed
250g (9oz) cavolo nero, tough stalks discarded,
  leaves chopped
8 ripe tomatoes, skinned, deseeded
  and quartered

1 dried chilli, crumbled (with seeds)
1.5 litres (2 1/2 pints) vegetable broth (page 47),
  or water
small handful of chopped flat leaf parsley
1 rosemary sprig, finely chopped
2 bay leaves
sea salt and freshly ground black pepper

TO SERVE:
8 slices of country-style bread
extra virgin olive oil (preferably new season's,
  estate bottled), to drizzle
3 tablespoons chopped flat leaf parsley

1 Drain the cannellini beans and rinse under fresh cold water. Place in a large saucepan, cover generously with cold water and bring to the boil. Lower the heat, cover and simmer gently for about 1 1/2 hours until the beans are just tender.

2 Heat half the olive oil in a large heavy-based pan, add the onion, cover and sweat for 5 minutes to soften. Add the carrots, celery, leeks and half of the garlic and sweat for a further 5 minutes. Add the cabbage, tomatoes and chilli and stir to coat in the oil. Add the beans and vegetable broth or water and simmer for 30 minutes or until the beans are soft.

3 Ladle a third of the soup mixture into a blender or food processor and whiz to a purée. Pour this back into the pan and stir to mix.

4 Heat the remaining 2 tablespoons olive oil in a separate pan and sauté the other crushed garlic clove with the chopped herbs and bay leaves until lightly browned. Add to the soup, allow to cool and refrigerate for 24 hours.

5 The next day, warm the soup through in an uncovered pan and check the seasoning. Place a slice of bread in each warm soup bowl and ladle the ribollita over the top. Drizzle with a generous amount of extra virgin olive oil and sprinkle with sea salt and chopped parsley to serve.

Italian broths

A good, fine flavoured *brodo* – broth or stock – is paramount in Italian cooking. It is the basis for most soups and savoury sauces, and is absolutely vital in the making of risottos. The ingredients, however, have to be of the finest quality.

A chicken broth really should be made with a good raw chicken, although a slightly less flavoursome broth can be made with a raw carcass (or you could use a cooked carcass if you have one leftover). A fish broth must be made with white fish bones, oily fish are not suitable. When you buy cleaned fish from the fishmonger or fresh fish counter, ask for the bones (and perhaps an extra white fish head or two for additional flavour).

With any of the following broths, the aromatic vegetables, herbs and spices can be varied to taste, but ideally you should use a flavouring base – or *soffritto* – of onion, celery, carrot and parsley.

▲ **fish broth**
To make about 1.2 litres (2 pints), put about 1kg (2¼lb) white fish heads and bones into a large saucepan. Add 2 peeled onions each stuck with 5 cloves, 2 carrots, 2 celery stalks, 2 bay leaves, 10 black peppercorns, 1½ teaspoons salt and 500ml (16fl oz) dry white wine. Add 2 litres (3½ pints) water and bring to the boil. Boil, uncovered, for 30 minutes until well reduced. Strain the liquid, discarding the bones and aromatics. Cool, then chill. Use within 1–2 days or freeze.

chicken broth

To make about 1.5 litres (2½ pints), rinse a 1.4kg (3lb) chicken in cold water and cut off any visible fat. Bring 3.4 litres (6 pints) water to the boil in a very large saucepan or stock pot over a high heat. Add the chicken to the pan along with 2 peeled onions, 2 celery stalks and 1 large potato, peeled and quartered. Add 3 bay leaves and a handful of parsley (leaves and stalks). Bring to the boil and boil rapidly for

▼ vegetable broth

To make about 1.5 litres (2½ pints), heat 1 tbsp olive oil with 40g (1½oz) unsalted butter in a large saucepan or stock pot. Add 3 crushed garlic cloves and fry gently for 2 minutes. Coarsely chop 1 large onion, 4 leeks, 2 carrots and 2 celery stalks. Add to the pan with 1 halved fennel bulb, a handful of chopped flat leaf parsley, 4 bay leaves, and 2 thyme sprigs. Cook over a low heat, stirring constantly, until softened, but

5 minutes. Reduce the heat to low and simmer very slowly, uncovered, for about 2 hours. Skim off any scum from the surface from time to time. Remove the chicken, then strain the broth through a fine sieve. Allow to cool, then chill the broth. Once chilled, remove the solidified fat that has accumulated on the surface. Keep refrigerated and use within 4–5 days, or freeze.

not browned. Add 3 litres (5 pints) water and bring to the boil. Reduce the heat, cover and simmer for 1 hour. Strain the stock and return to the pan, discarding the solids. Boil rapidly until reduced by half. Allow to cool. Keep refrigerated and use within 3 days, or freeze.

fennel soup with roasted tomatoes

In the high bleak mountains of Sardinia, the wild greens and herbs that grow in abundance everywhere are used in cooking, both by the itinerant shepherds, and in Sardinian homes. Small wild fennel bulbs are traditional here, but cultivated fennel works perfectly well.
Illustrated on previous page

SERVES 4

4 fennel bulbs
1 tablespoon olive oil
1.5 litres (2½ pints) vegetable broth (page 47)
1 teaspoon fennel seeds
handful of flat leaf parsley, finely chopped
sea salt and freshly ground black pepper
TO SERVE:
200g (7oz) roasted cherry tomatoes (page 36)

1 Trim the fennel bulbs, reserving the feathery fronds and discarding the stalks and tough outer layers. Slice the bulbs thinly, then chop finely. Chop the feathery tops as well; set aside.

2 Heat the olive oil in a large pan, add the chopped fennel and cook over a low heat for 10 minutes. Add the broth, fennel seeds and seasoning. Bring to the boil and simmer for 30 minutes.

3 Stir in the chopped parsley and ladle the soup into warm bowls. Top with the roasted cherry tomatoes and fennel fronds to serve.

onion and chick pea soup

This tasty soup of onions, chick peas, tomatoes, bacon and bread originates from the Marches. It keeps well and tastes even better a day or two after it is made.

SERVES 6

200g (7oz) dried chick peas, soaked overnight
300g (11oz) ripe tomatoes
4 tablespoons olive oil
1kg (2¼lb) onions, peeled and sliced
1 celery stalk, chopped
50g (2oz) unsmoked bacon, diced
handful of basil leaves, torn
6 slices of firm, coarse-textured bread
sea salt and freshly ground black pepper

1 Drain and rinse the chick peas. Purée the tomatoes through a food mill or in a blender, then sieve.

2 Heat the olive oil in a large saucepan, add the onions, celery and bacon and fry gently for about 5 minutes until the onion is translucent. Add the puréed tomatoes, chick peas and 2 litres (3½ pints) water. Bring to the boil, lower the heat and simmer for 2 hours. Season and add add most of the basil.

3 When ready to serve, toast the bread slices on both sides and place a slice in each warm soup bowl. Pour the hot soup on top and sprinkle with the remaining torn basil.

farro and bean soup

Farro, a form of spelt or soft wheat, is an ancient grain, which was grown and eaten by the Romans. It is now mainly cultivated in the Garfagnana region of Tuscany, where this protein-rich soup originated. Farro has a great texture which readily absorbs flavours, such as the *soffritto* (flavouring base) of carrot, celery and onion. Combined with borlotti beans, it makes for a wonderfully satisfying soup.

SERVES 6

250g (9oz) dried borlotti beans, soaked in cold
  water overnight
200g (7oz) farro, soaked in cold water overnight
2 white onions, peeled
6 sage leaves
3 garlic cloves, peeled
4 tablespoons olive oil

1 red onion, peeled and finely chopped
2 carrots, scraped and diced
2–4 celery stalks, trimmed and diced
handful of flat leaf parsley, chopped
275g (10oz) canned Italian plum tomatoes, with
  their juice
sea salt and freshly ground black pepper
extra virgin olive oil, to drizzle

1   Drain and rinse the borlotti beans, then place in a large saucepan with 1 whole white onion, 3 sage leaves, 1 garlic clove and enough water to cover by at least 5cm (2 inches). Bring to the boil, lower the heat, cover and simmer for 1 hour or until tender.

2   When the beans are cooked, pass half of the contents of the pan through a food mill or purée in a blender or food processor and set aside. Keep the whole beans in the pan.

3   Finely chop the other white onion and the remaining garlic. Heat the olive oil in a large saucepan, add the chopped red and white onion, the carrots, celery and garlic. Stir well, then add most of the parsley, the remaining 3 sage leaves, tomatoes and 3 tablespoons water. Continue to cook, stirring occasionally, for 10 minutes.

4   Drain and rinse the farro and add to the tomato mixture along with the whole borlotti beans. Bring to a simmer and simmer over a low heat for 20 minutes. Add the puréed bean mixture and season with salt and pepper. Heat, stirring, until thoroughly warmed through.

5   Taste and adjust the seasoning and ladle into warm bowls. Serve topped with a generous drizzle of extra virgin olive oil and the remaining chopped parsley.

Livorno fish soup

Livorno is a city by the sea in Tuscany, famous for its beautiful 17th century port. It is also renowned for its robust fish soup or stew, which is made from a variety of Mediterranean fish.

SERVES 6

4 tablespoons olive oil

1 onion, peeled and finely chopped

1 carrot, peeled and finely chopped

1 celery stalk, finely chopped

handful of flat leaf parsley, chopped

small piece of hot red chilli, very finely chopped

500g (1lb 2oz) raw prawns in shell

2 medium squid, cleaned and sliced into rings

250ml (8fl oz) dry white wine

300g (11oz) plum tomatoes, skinned and chopped

500g (1lb 2oz) fresh mussels, cleaned

500g (1lb 2oz) fresh clams, cleaned

650g (1lb 7oz) sea bream, filleted and skinned

1 small cooked lobster, cleaned (optional)

salt and freshly ground black pepper

TO SERVE:

6 thin slices of firm, coarse-textured bread

2 garlic cloves, peeled and crushed

1 Heat the olive oil in a large pan, add the onion, carrot, celery, parsley and chilli, and cook over a medium heat until the onion begins to colour. Stir in the prawns and squid and cook gently for 10 minutes, then remove the prawns and set aside. Add the wine, 125ml (4fl oz) hot water and the tomatoes and simmer for a further 10 minutes. Season with salt. Remove the squid and set aside.

2 Put the mussels and clams into a steamer over boiling water, cover tightly and steam just until open, about 3–5 minutes. Discard any that remain closed.

3 Meanwhile, strain the vegetables and cooking liquor through a fine sieve into a saucepan, rubbing with the back of a ladle. Add the bream fillets and simmer until opaque, about 4–5 minutes. Add all the seafood to the pan, including the lobster if using. Heat through gently and check the seasoning. In the meantime, toast the bread slices and spread with the garlic. Place in warm soup bowls, ladle the fish soup over the garlic toasts and serve.

chicken soup with poached egg and Parmesan

Known as *zuppa alla pavese*, this dish comes from Padua – Romeo and Juliet country. It is a great soup for a cold winter's evening – substantial, interesting, and very tasty. A good homemade broth is essential.

SERVES 6

1.5 litres (2½ pints) chicken broth (page 47)
1 bay leaf
6 thin slices of day-old, coarse-textured bread
6 eggs
sea salt and freshly ground black pepper

TO SERVE:
handful of flat leaf parsley, finely chopped
50g (2oz) Parmesan cheese, freshly grated
freshly grated nutmeg, to taste

1   Heat the chicken broth in a large, wide pan. Add the bay leaf and simmer gently over a medium heat for 10 minutes, then discard the bay leaf and check the seasoning. In the meantime, toast the bread slices.

2   One at a time, break the eggs into a cup and gently pour into the hot broth. The egg whites will immediately coagulate. Continue to poach until the whites are set.

3   Put a slice of toasted bread into each warm soup bowl. Using a slotted spoon, carefully place a poached egg on top, then ladle in the fragrant broth. Scatter the parsley and Parmesan on top and sprinkle with a little grated nutmeg. Serve at once.

lentil soup with pancetta and potatoes

This flavoursome soup of lentils, pancetta, potatoes, parsley and tomatoes is wonderfully enticing. I would always use Castelluccio lentils, which are hand-grown and picked in Italy. However, as an alternative, you can use the French Puy lentils, which lend a slightly different texture and flavour.

SERVES 6

10 new potatoes, preferably Italian, scrubbed
3 bay leaves
100g (3½oz) pancetta, diced
2 garlic cloves, peeled and crushed
225g (8oz) small green lentils
3 tablespoons olive oil
700g jar tomato passata, or 2 x 400g cans
    chopped tomatoes
sea salt and freshly ground black pepper

TO SERVE:

50g (2oz) Parmesan cheese, freshly grated
generous handful of flat leaf parsley, chopped
extra virgin olive oil, to drizzle

1 Cut the potatoes into even-sized cubes and put into a medium saucepan. Pour in 900ml (1½ pints) boiling water and add the bay leaves, salt and pepper. Bring to a simmer and cook for 10 minutes.

2 In the meantime, fry the pancetta dice in a dry frying pan over a medium heat, turning frequently, until golden.

3 Add the pancetta to the potatoes, with the garlic, lentils, olive oil, passata or chopped tomatoes, and some pepper. Return to a simmer, cover and cook for 40 minutes. Adjust the seasoning.

4 Serve sprinkled with Parmesan and parsley, and topped with a generous drizzle of good, fruity extra virgin olive oil.

potato and sausage soup

This comforting, hearty soup comes from Emilia-Romagna, the gastronomic centre of Italy. It is made from a purée of potatoes and onions, with the addition of sausage. The semolina shouldn't be omitted as it adds a good texture, but you can vary the flavour by using different types of sausages. Freshly grated Parmesan and plenty of parsley are essential.

SERVES 6

1.5 litres (2½ pints) chicken broth (page 47)
3 medium potatoes, peeled and sliced
1 onion, peeled and finely chopped
125ml (4fl oz) milk
1 tablespoon semolina
2 cooked Italian sausages, thinly sliced
sea salt and freshly ground black pepper

TO SERVE:

handful of flat leaf parsley, finely chopped
freshly grated Parmesan cheese, to taste

1 Heat the chicken broth in a large saucepan, then add the sliced potatoes and onion. Cook over a medium heat for 10–15 minutes or until the potato is soft.

2 Using a slotted spoon, remove the potato and onion from the stock and pass through a food mill, or mash until smooth, then return to the liquid.

3 Add the milk and sprinkle the semolina over the soup, stirring constantly. Cook over a medium heat, stirring, for 10 minutes. Add the sausage slices and cook for a further 10 minutes. Season with salt and pepper to taste.

4 Ladle the soup into warm bowls and scatter over the parsley. Sprinkle with Parmesan and serve.

3 breads and pizzas

ciabatta

Olive oil enriched, crisp and flavourful, this is the bread that all bakers aspire to make, yet it really is quite simple. The starting point is a 'biga', a fermented yeast starter, which makes the dough sweeter and smoother, and gives the loaf its characteristic open texture.

MAKES 4 LOAVES

7g (1/4oz) fresh yeast, or 1 teaspoon fast-action
* dried yeast*
500g (1lb 2oz) strong white bread flour
15g (1/2oz) sea salt
500g (1lb 2oz) biga (see right)
olive oil, to oil

1 Measure 300ml (1/2 pint) warm water in a jug. In a small bowl, blend the fresh yeast (or simply mix the dried yeast) with 3 tablespoons of this water.

2 Combine the flour and salt in a large bowl, make a well in the centre and add the biga, yeast liquid and water. Mix together to form a sticky dough, then knead well to develop the elasticity. As it is wet, the dough will continually adhere to your hand in large elastic lumps, but persevere, or use a mixer to knead it if you prefer. Do the stretch test (see below) to check the dough is ready.

3 Liberally oil a large bowl, drop in the dough and turn it carefully to bathe in olive oil. Leave in a warm place until doubled or even trebled in volume, 1 1/2–2 hours or possibly even longer.

4 Oil two baking trays. Gently ease the puffy dough on to a well floured surface, avoiding knocking it down. With floured hands and a dough scraper or sharp knife, cut into 4 pieces. As you pick each piece up, gently roll in the flour and give it a hearty stretch to elongate it to the classic slipper shape, then place on the baking trays. Cover and leave to prove for an hour.

5 Meanwhile, preheat the oven to 200°C (fan oven 180°C), gas mark 6. After proving the loaves will still look flat, but they will spring up in the oven. Bake them for 20 minutes until golden. Cool on a wire rack and eat warm.

stretch test   To check whether a dough has been kneaded enough for the gluten to develop elasticity, stretch a piece of dough between your fingers. It should behave like an elastic band, not ripping or breaking. This is what I call 'the stretch test', vital when making breads.

biga

This fermented yeast starter is the cornerstone of Italian breads. It enhances the performance of the yeast in the dough, helps to develop that wonderful yeasty aroma and gives a characteristic open texture. Use fresh yeast if possible. You won't use all of the biga for the ciabatta or any of my other breads, but you can keep the rest in the refrigerator to make another loaf – for up to 3 days (no longer, or it will become acidic).

MAKES ABOUT 1kg (2¼lb)

7g (¼oz) fresh yeast, or 1 teaspoon fast-action
  dried yeast
575g (1¼ lb) strong white bread flour

1   Measure 400ml (14fl oz) warm water in a jug. In a small bowl, blend the fresh yeast (or simply mix dried yeast) with a little of this water.

2   Mix all the biga ingredients together in a large bowl and beat with a spoon or your hands until you have a smooth, loose dough. You should feel the elasticity as the gluten develops. Cover and leave to stand at room temperature for 12–24 hours.

olive and rosemary focaccia

This Italian classic bread is flavoured with caramelised onion and garlic, and topped with olives, sea salt and rosemary before baking. It is best served warm, drizzled with new season's olive oil.

MAKES 1 LARGE LOAF

2 large rosemary sprigs

2 tablespoons olive oil

1 onion, peeled, halved and sliced

2 garlic cloves, peeled and finely chopped

10 black olives, pitted and halved
   lengthways

sea salt and coarsely ground black pepper

FOR THE DOUGH:

7g (¼oz) fresh yeast, or 1 teaspoon fast-action
   dried yeast

275g (10oz) strong white flour

1 teaspoon sea salt

25g (1oz) wholemeal flour

100g (3½oz) biga (page 61)

olive oil, to oil

1 Finely chop a third of the rosemary leaves; keep another third of them whole; divide the rest into tiny sprigs and set aside for the topping. Heat the olive oil in a frying pan and sauté the onion and chopped rosemary for 10 minutes. Add the garlic and cook over a medium heat until the mixture caramelises. Tip into a bowl and cool.

2 For the dough, dissolve the yeast in 225ml (7½fl oz) warm water. Mix the white flour with the sea salt on the work surface, pile into a mound and make a well in the centre. Add the wholemeal flour, biga and yeast liquid to the well, then gradually draw in the white flour with your hands and mix to a dough, adding a little extra water if necessary.

3 Knead the dough for 10 minutes until smooth and elastic, then add half the caramelised onion and continue to knead for 10 minutes. Do the stretch test to check that the dough is ready (see page 60). Place in a lightly oiled large bowl and turn the dough to coat. Cover with a tea towel and leave in a warm place for 2 hours or until almost doubled in bulk.

4 Tip the dough out on to a lightly floured surface and gently knead into a round ball. Place on a well oiled large baking tray. Cover and allow to rest for 15 minutes, then flatten the dough with the palm of your hand to a 20cm (8 inch) round.

5 Mix the rosemary leaves with the remaining onion mixture and spread evenly over the surface of the dough. Season generously with pepper. Cover to prevent a skin forming and leave to prove for 2 hours.

6 Preheat the oven to 200°C (fan oven 180°C), gas mark 6. Stud the dough with the olives and scatter with sea salt. Bake for 15–18 minutes until golden. Transfer to a wire rack to cool slightly and serve warm, scattered with rosemary sprigs.

semolina bread rolls

These rolls come from Puglia in southern Italy. Semolina gives a rich colour and a slightly grainy texture and crust. Flavour the dough with a handful of chopped fresh herbs (or a sprinkling of dried) if you like. Perfect for breakfast, these rolls also make delicious *panini* (pages 68–9).

MAKES 12 ROLLS

7g (¼oz) fresh yeast, or 1 teaspoon fast-action
  dried yeast
375g (13oz) strong white flour
275g (10oz) semolina

2 teaspoons coarsely ground black pepper
125g (4oz) biga (page 61)
15g (½oz) sea salt
olive oil, to oil
2 tablespoons coarse sea salt, to sprinkle

1 Dissolve the yeast in 375ml (13fl oz) warm water. Combine the flour, semolina and black pepper on a work surface and pile into a mound. Make a well in the centre and add the yeast water and biga. Mix with your hand until all the ingredients are well combined – this will take about 5 minutes.

2 Add the sea salt and knead the dough for 10 minutes until smooth and elastic. Do the stretch test to check that the dough is ready (see page 60). Place the dough in a lightly oiled large bowl, cover with cling film and leave in a warm place until doubled in size, approximately 2 hours.

3 Knock back the dough in the bowl, re-cover and leave to rise again for 45 minutes. This second rising will give the dough more strength.

4 Tip the dough on to a lightly floured surface and cut into 12 pieces, using a dough scraper or sharp knife. Shape into balls, place on a lightly oiled baking tray and leave to prove for another hour.

5 Preheat the oven to 200°C (fan oven 180°C), gas mark 6. Using a sharp knife, cut a cross on top of each roll, then sprinkle liberally with coarse salt. Bake for 20 minutes, opening the oven door slightly for the last 5 minutes – this makes the rolls crisper. Cool on a wire rack and eat warm.

honey bread

Sweetened with honey and dried fruit, and enriched with eggs, this bread will keep well for a day or two. The combination of honey and aniseed is a good one, but you can leave out the aniseed if you're not keen on the taste. Delicious at teatime, this sweet bread toasts well too.

MAKES 1 LARGE LOAF

15g (1/2oz) fresh yeast, or 2 teaspoons fast-action dried yeast
275ml (9fl oz) warm whole milk
175ml (6fl oz) thin honey
2 tablespoons melted unsalted butter, cooled
2 tablespoons olive oil, plus extra to oil
1 large egg, beaten
1/2 tablespoon sea salt

2 tablespoons aniseed seeds
1 tablespoon finely grated unwaxed lemon zest
450g (1lb) strong white flour, plus extra if needed

FOR THE FILLING AND TOPPING:
50g (2oz) raisins
50g (2oz) shelled walnuts, finely chopped
50g (2oz) pitted prunes, finely chopped
3 tablespoons thin honey

1 Dissolve the yeast in 125ml (4fl oz) warm water in a large bowl, then leave for 10 minutes.

2 Add the milk, 175ml (6fl oz) honey, the melted butter, olive oil, egg, salt, aniseed and lemon zest to the yeast liquid and stir well.

3 Add the flour and mix with your hands to obtain a ball of dough. If the dough is sticky, mix in a little extra flour. Knead well for 10 minutes to form a soft, smooth, elastic dough. Do the stretch test (see page 60) to check that it is ready. Cover and leave to rise for 1 1/2 hours or until doubled in size.

4 In a small bowl, mix together the raisins, walnuts and prunes. Punch back the dough and turn it out on to a floured surface. Knead for 2–3 minutes, then roll out to a 40cm (16 inch) round. Using a brush, spread 2 tablespoons of the honey over the dough and sprinkle with three-quarters of the fruit and nut mixture.

5 Roll the dough up to enclose the filling and form a 40cm (16 inch) long loaf, about 7.5cm (3 inches) thick. Press the ends together to seal, or the honey will seep out. Lift on to a lightly oiled baking tray, cover and set aside to prove for 40–60 minutes.

6 Meanwhile, preheat the oven to 200°C (fan oven 180°C), gas mark 6. Bake the loaf for 30 minutes until the crust is golden brown. Transfer to a wire rack and brush with the remaining honey, then sprinkle the rest of the nut and fruit mixture on top. Cool before serving.

panini

Bread is the 'staff of life' in Italy, and to describe someone as *buono come il pane* – as good, kind, warm-hearted and generous as bread – is a great compliment! It plays a part in virtually every Italian meal, but also figures throughout the day: a panino might be eaten instead of breakfast, for example, or as a mid-morning or afternoon snack.

Panino literally means a bread roll, but nowadays it usually refers to a filled roll, a *panino imbottito*, and anything less like a typical British sandwich would be hard to imagine. An Italian *panino* is a truly wonderful marriage of tasty filling ingredients and irresistible crisp, crusty bread. It is either eaten cold or hot – after warming in a salamander or in a low oven.

Ciabatta loaves and rolls, available from most supermarkets, are convenient bases for *panini*, but you could also use sfilatino or focaccia, or homemade breads, such as the semolina rolls on page 64.

▲ **mozzarella and baby spinach ciabatta**
To serve 2, cut a half ciabatta loaf in two, then split each horizontally. Moisten the insides with extra virgin olive oil. Lay 3 baby spinach leaves on each ciabatta base and add 6 pitted black olives and 2 thin slices of red onion. Cover with 2 generous slices of buffalo mozzarella and 3 drained anchovy fillets in oil. Top with another 3 spinach leaves and season with salt and pepper. Cover with the tops and press down lightly. Heat to serve if required.

Taleggio, artichoke and rocket ciabatta

To serve 4–5, split a whole ciabatta loaf in half horizontally and drizzle the cut surfaces with extra virgin olive oil. Layer 250g (9oz) thinly sliced Taleggio cheese on the base and top with a handful of rocket leaves. Cover with 150g (5oz) drained, sliced artichoke hearts (in oil). Season well. Position the top of the loaf and press down lightly. Heat through if liked. Cut into sections.

cherry tomato, red onion and speck panini

To serve 1, divide a ciabatta roll in half and moisten the insides with extra virgin olive oil. Place 4 halved cherry tomatoes on the base and top with ¼ red onion, thinly sliced. Cover with 2 slices speck (smoked, salt-cured, air-dried ham). Finish with 3 slices of smoked scamorza cheese (or mozzarella). Season generously with pepper, but lightly with salt. Position the top of the roll, press down lightly and heat if liked.

▲ prosciutto, roasted pepper and radicchio panini

To serve 1, split a ciabatta roll in half and moisten the cut surfaces with extra virgin olive oil. Layer torn radicchio leaves and two thin slices of fontina cheese on the base, and add some wild rocket leaves and roasted red pepper slices (bought from the deli counter). Add 2 thin slices prosciutto, loosely folded, and season generously. Position the top part of the roll and press down lightly. Heat through if liked.

pizza dough base

Pizzas were first created in Naples, essentially as street food. Even today, the best pizzas are still made in the south, where local wheat and water produce the finest texture and crust. The best type of flour to use is Italian '0' grade (not the '00' type used for pasta, which isn't suitable).

Basically a pizza is a flat bread, used as a base for toppings which range from the simplest marinara (see right) to many more sophisticated concoctions. In Italy, pizzas are a serious business. There are rules and standards, and every *pizzaiola* (pizza-maker) must possess a licence from the government to ensure that he satisfies these.

MAKES TWO 25CM (10 INCH) PIZZA BASES

15g (1/2oz) fresh yeast, or 11/2 teaspoons fast-
  action dried yeast
250g (9oz) strong white unbleached flour
1/2 teaspoon sea salt
50ml (2fl oz) olive oil, plus extra to oil
semolina, to sprinkle

1 Measure 50ml (2fl oz) warm water in a jug. Blend the fresh yeast (or simply mix dried yeast) with a little of this water.

2 Sift the flour and salt together into a large bowl. Make a well in the centre and add the olive oil, yeast liquid and some of the water. Mix together with a wooden spoon, gradually adding the remaining water, to form a soft dough.

3 Turn the dough out on to a lightly floured surface and knead vigorously for 10 minutes until it is soft and satiny (don't be afraid of adding more flour). Place in a lightly oiled large bowl, then turn the dough around to coat with the oil. Cover the bowl with a clean tea towel and leave in a warm place for 11/2 hours, or until the dough has doubled in size.

4 Preheat the oven to 200°C (fan oven 180°C), gas mark 6. In the bottom of the oven, preheat two oiled baking sheets or a terracotta pizza stone. Knock down the dough with your knuckles, then turn on to a lightly floured surface and knead for 2–3 minutes to knock out the air bubbles. Divide the dough in half.

5 On a lightly floured surface, preferably marble, roll out the pieces of dough very, very thinly, until 25–30cm (10–12 inches) in diameter. (They should be as thin as a paper napkin folded in four.) Now lift each pizza base on to a cold baking sheet sprinkled generously with semolina (this will make it easier to slide the pizza off). Add your chosen topping.

6 Lightly oil the preheated baking sheets. Carefully slide the prepared pizzas off the cold baking sheets directly on to the hot baking sheets or pizza stone and immediately bake in the oven for 20–25 minutes until golden and crisp.

pizza marinara

This is the original, simple tomato pizza. Purists in Naples claim there are only two authentic pizzas: the marinara and the margarita. I favour the marinara because I love its fresh taste and simplicity. For extra flavour, you might like to scatter some anchovies on top before baking.

SERVES 2
1 quantity pizza dough (page 70)
4–5 fresh plum tomatoes, skinned
6–8 basil leaves, torn

1 garlic clove, peeled and chopped
3 teaspoons dried oregano
sea salt and freshly ground black pepper
extra virgin olive oil, to drizzle

1 Preheat the oven to 200°C (fan oven 180°C), gas mark 6, and preheat two baking sheets or a pizza stone. On a lightly floured surface, roll out the pizza dough very thinly into two 25–30cm (10–12 inch) rounds, then lift each pizza base on to a cold baking sheet sprinkled with semolina (see page 70).

2 Put the tomatoes, basil and seasoning in a blender or food processor and whiz to a purée, or pass through a food mill. Spread this tomato sauce over the pizza bases and top with the garlic and oregano.

3 Slide the pizzas on to the oiled hot baking sheets and bake for about 20 minutes until the crust is crisp and golden brown. Drizzle with extra virgin olive oil to serve.

pizza margarita

I love simple food: good ingredients, carefully combined and used at their freshest, are a joy. This fresh tomato and mozzarella pizza couldn't be more straightforward. For the best flavour, choose bright red, ripe tomatoes with a distinctive peppery aroma (detected at the stalk end).

SERVES 4–6
1 quantity pizza dough (page 70)
large handful of basil leaves, torn
675g (1¹/₂lb) cherry tomatoes, halved

small handful of oregano leaves, chopped
250g (9oz) mozzarella cheese, grated
sea salt and freshly ground black pepper

1 Preheat the oven to 200°C (fan oven 180°C), gas mark 6, and preheat two baking sheets or a pizza stone. On a lightly floured surface, roll out the dough very thinly into two 25–30cm (10–12 inch) rounds. Now lift each pizza base on to a cold baking sheet sprinkled with semolina (see page 70).

2 Scatter the basil leaves over the pizza bases, then add the cherry tomato halves, chopped oregano, salt, pepper and grated mozzarella.

3 Slide the pizzas on to the oiled hot baking sheets and bake for about 20 minutes until the tomatoes are softened and the cheese is bubbling and golden.

pizza with aubergine and ricotta

I love aubergines and this is one of my favourite ways of eating them. Although not everyone does so, I always salt and rinse aubergines before cooking them. First and foremost, salting draws out beads of bitter juices; and secondly, the aubergines will absorb less oil afterwards.
Illustrated on previous page

SERVES 2
1 quantity pizza dough (page 70)
1 medium aubergine
3 tablespoons olive oil
1 small red onion, peeled and sliced into rings
4 ripe tomatoes, skinned and sliced
25g (1oz) Parmesan cheese, freshly grated
250g (9oz) ricotta cheese
good handful of basil leaves
sea salt and freshly ground black pepper

1 Wrap the pizza dough in cling film and set aside until you are ready to roll out. Slice the aubergine lengthways, then put the slices into a colander, sprinkle with salt, cover and weight down. Leave for 30 minutes to degorge the bitter juices.

2 Preheat the oven to 200°C (fan oven 180°C), gas mark 6, and preheat two baking sheets or a pizza stone. Preheat the grill to medium.

3 Heat a third of the olive oil in a saucepan, add the onion rings and fry until softened. Add the tomatoes, salt and pepper and set aside.

4 Rinse the aubergine slices to remove the salt and pat dry. Brush them with half the remaining olive oil and grill for 5 minutes on each side until lightly cooked.

5 On a lightly floured surface, roll out the pizza dough very thinly into two 25–30cm (10–12 inch) rounds. Now lift each pizza base on to a cold baking sheet sprinkled with semolina (see page 70). Brush with the remaining olive oil, then spread with the tomato mixture. Sprinkle over the Parmesan cheese and add the ricotta. Arrange the aubergine slices on top, radiating from the centre, then tuck some of the basil leaves under the slices.

6 Slide the pizzas on to the oiled hot baking sheets and bake for 20–25 minutes until golden and bubbling. Serve hot, scattered with the rest of the basil leaves.

pizza norcina

I first enjoyed this pizza in Norcina, in Umbria, a region famous for its truffles. It tasted so good that I returned the following day for another. Truffle hunting is taken very seriously in Umbria: a good truffle is a real prize and it becomes a talking point for months on end. Here I have used truffle paste, made from a combination of truffle and porcini mushrooms, and available in jars.

SERVES 2

1 quantity pizza dough (page 70)
25g (1oz) dried porcini mushrooms
250g (9oz) large flat mushrooms, wiped
2 tablespoons olive oil
1 garlic clove, peeled and crushed
250g (9oz) mozzarella cheese, grated
25g (1oz) truffle paste (salsina)
sea salt and freshly ground black pepper

1 Wrap the pizza dough in cling film and set aside until ready to roll out. Preheat the oven to 200°C (fan oven 180°C), gas mark 6, and preheat two baking sheets or a pizza stone.

2 Soak the dried porcini in warm water to cover for about 20 minutes, then drain and pat dry. Slice the fresh mushrooms.

3 Heat the olive oil in a frying pan, add the porcini and sliced fresh mushrooms and fry until softened. Add the garlic and some salt and pepper.

4 On a lightly floured surface, roll out the pizza dough very thinly into two 25–30cm (10–12 inch) rounds. Now lift each pizza base on to a cold baking sheet sprinkled with semolina (see page 70). Top the pizza bases with the mushrooms and mozzarella, then add little mounds of truffle paste.

5 Slide the pizzas on to the oiled hot baking sheets, and bake for 20–25 minutes until golden and bubbling. Serve immediately.

asparagus calzone

To make calzone, you simply fold the pizza dough over the filling and seal the edges, like a pasty. Here, the sweet, succulent flavour and aroma of fresh asparagus is held within, until you cut into the calzone. Make this in early summer, when young, homegrown asparagus is in season.

SERVES 2
1 quantity pizza dough (page 70)
2 tender, young courgettes
300g (11oz) asparagus spears

150g (5oz) ricotta cheese
1 tablespoon freshly grated Parmesan cheese
2 tablespoons olive oil
sea salt and freshly ground black pepper

1   Wrap the pizza dough in cling film and set aside until ready to roll out. Preheat the oven to 200°C (fan oven 180°C), gas mark 6, and preheat a baking sheet or a pizza stone. Slice the courgettes, place in a colander and sprinkle with salt. Leave for 20 minutes, then rinse under cold water and pat dry.

2   Cut off the pale stalk ends and peel the lower end of the asparagus stalks, using a swivel vegetable peeler. Add the asparagus spears to a saucepan of boiling water, return to the boil, then immediately drain and rinse under cold water. Cut into 5cm (2 inch) pieces and pat dry.

3   Put the asparagus, courgettes, ricotta and Parmesan into a bowl. Mix together and season with salt and pepper to taste. Stir in 1 tablespoon olive oil.

4   On a lightly floured surface, roll out the pizza dough into two 25–30cm (10–12 inch) rounds. Now lift each round on to a cold baking sheet sprinkled with semolina (see page 70). Pile the filling on one side of each round, moisten the edge with water and bring the uncovered side over the filling. Using your fingers, press the edges together to seal, fold them up and crimp.

5   Brush the calzone with the remaining olive oil, slide on to the hot oiled baking sheet and bake for 20–25 minutes until golden brown. Allow to stand for 10 minutes before serving.

gorgonzola and artichoke pizza

This versatile pizza can be served hot straight from the oven, or cold for a picnic. Canned artichokes are a great storecupboard standby and a convenient alternative to preparing fresh artichoke hearts. For this recipe, I roast them first before arranging on the pizza.

SERVES 2

1 quantity pizza dough (page 70)
6 canned artichoke hearts
3 tablespoons olive oil
150g (5oz) mozzarella cheese, grated
150g (5oz) Gorgonzola cheese, sliced
3 tablespoons Parmesan cheese, freshly grated
1 tablespoon pine nuts, toasted
1 teaspoon finely chopped sage
sea salt and freshly ground black pepper

1 Wrap the pizza dough in cling film and set aside until ready to roll out. Preheat the oven to 200°C (fan oven 180°C), gas mark 6, and preheat two baking sheets or a pizza stone.

2 Rinse the artichokes well, pat dry and place in a small roasting tin. Drizzle with the olive oil and roast in the oven for 10 minutes until golden. Transfer to a board and cut into quarters.

3 On a lightly floured surface, roll out the pizza dough very thinly into two 25–30cm (10–12 inch) rounds. Now lift each pizza base on to a cold baking sheet sprinkled with semolina (see page 70).

4 Scatter the mozzarella and Gorgonzola on top of the pizza bases and arrange the artichoke hearts on top. Sprinkle over the Parmesan, pine nuts and sage, and season with salt and pepper.

5 Slide the pizzas on to the oiled hot baking sheets and bake for 20–25 minutes until golden and bubbling. Eat hot or cold.

spinach, olive and onion testo

I first enjoyed this *testo* in Naples airport. Baked as a large flat round, the olive oil enriched dough has a tasty spinach, mozzarella and olive filling in the middle. It is cut into wedges to serve, and I like to take it on picnics.

MAKES 1

FOR THE DOUGH:
15g (1/2oz) fresh yeast, or 1 1/2 teaspoons fast
   action dried yeast
500g (1lb 2oz) strong white unbleached flour
2 teaspoons sea salt
3 tablespoons olive oil

FOR THE FILLING:
2 tablespoons olive oil
1 large red onion, peeled and sliced
1 garlic clove, peeled and crushed
1/2 dried long, thin red chilli (peperoncini), crushed
750g (1lb 10oz) spinach, trimmed, washed and
   finely chopped
125g (4oz) pitted green olives
75g (3oz) mozzarella cheese, chopped
sea salt and freshly ground black pepper

TO FINISH:
olive oil, to drizzle
coarse sea salt, to sprinkle

1 First prepare the dough. Measure 275ml (9fl oz) warm water in a jug. Mix the yeast with 1 tablespoon of the water. Put the flour and salt into a large bowl and mix well together. Make a well in the middle and pour in the yeast liquid, the olive oil and some of the remaining water. Mix together, gradually adding the rest of the measured water, to form a soft dough.

2 Turn the dough on to a lightly floured work surface and knead vigorously for 10 minutes until smooth. Return the dough to a clean bowl, cover with a cloth and leave in a warm place for 45 minutes until doubled in size.

3 Knead the risen dough again for 1–2 minutes to knock out the air bubbles. Return to the bowl, cover and leave to rise for about 40 minutes.

4 For the filling, heat the olive oil in a large frying pan. Add the onion, garlic and chilli, and cook for about 5 minutes. Add the spinach and cook for another 5 minutes until it is wilted. Take off the heat, add the olives and season with salt and pepper. Allow to cool, then mix in the mozzarella.

5 Divide the dough in half. Roll out each piece on a lightly floured surface to a 33cm (13 inch) round. Place one round on a lightly oiled baking sheet and spoon the filling on top, leaving a margin around the edge. Dampen the edge, cover with the second round of dough and pinch the edges together to seal. Leave to prove for 30 minutes. Preheat the oven to 200°C (fan oven 180°C), gas mark 6.

6 Drizzle the testo with olive oil and sprinkle with sea salt. Bake for 25 minutes, then transfer to a wire rack. Serve hot, warm or cold, cut into wedges.

4 pasta, polenta and rice

parsley pasta with clams and black olives

Linguine and trenette are similar long, thin ribbon pasta, rather like flattened spaghetti. I like to serve this fine pasta with an unusual clam and olive sauce, inspired by a similar dish that I enjoyed on the Sardinian coast. The small, sweet Venus clams are my favourite.

SERVES 4

350g (12oz) dried linguine or trenette pasta
very large handful of flat leaf parsley,
* finely chopped*
3 tablespoons extra virgin olive oil
sea salt and freshly ground black pepper

FOR THE CLAM SAUCE:

10 ripe plum tomatoes
2 tablespoons olive oil
3 garlic cloves, peeled and chopped
40 fresh clams
1 celery stalk, very finely chopped
20 Gaeta olives, pitted
175ml (6fl oz) dry white wine
handful of basil leaves, roughly torn

1 For the sauce, immerse the tomatoes in a bowl of boiling hot water for 10 seconds to loosen the skins, then drain and peel away the skins. Chop the tomato flesh. Heat the olive oil in a large heavy-based sauté pan. Add the garlic and sauté over a medium heat until very lightly golden. Add the clams, cover the pan with a tight-fitting lid and cook over a high heat for 4–6 minutes until the shells have opened. Discard any clams that remain closed.

2 Meanwhile, add the pasta to a large pan of boiling salted water and cook at a fast boil until *al dente* (tender but firm to the bite).

3 Add the tomatoes, celery, olives and wine to the clams and cook until the wine evaporates, about 1 minute. Season with salt and pepper to taste and scatter in the torn basil. Take off the heat.

4 Drain the pasta well and toss with the parsley and extra virgin olive oil. Combine with the clam sauce, and eat straightaway.

pasta 'Norma'

This dish is thought to have been invented by a Sicilian chef, for the first performance of Bellini's opera 'Norma' to be performed on the island. It is a typical southern Italian pasta dish – colourful, with robust flavours. When fresh plum tomatoes are out of season, use canned tomatoes; the basil flavoured variety works well here.

SERVES 6

1kg (2¼lb) fresh plum tomatoes, or
  2 x 400g cans chopped tomatoes
5 tablespoons olive oil
1 onion, peeled and finely chopped
2 garlic cloves, peeled and crushed

2 medium aubergines, trimmed
450–500g (1lb–1lb 2oz) penne rigate (quills
  with ridges)
handful of small basil leaves
sea salt and freshly ground black pepper
freshly grated Parmesan cheese, to serve

1   If using fresh tomatoes, plunge them into boiling water for 10 seconds, then drain and peel away the skins. Quarter the tomatoes and remove the cores. Heat 2 tablespoons olive oil in a large saucepan, add the onion and sauté for a few minutes to soften. Add the crushed garlic and sauté for a minute or two, then add the prepared fresh or canned tomatoes and season well with salt and pepper. Cover and cook for 25 minutes.

2   Meanwhile, slice the aubergines lengthways into strips, 2cm (¾ inch) long. Sprinkle with salt, place in a bowl or colander and weight down. Leave to degorge their bitter juices for 20 minutes. Rinse the aubergine strips thoroughly and pat dry.

3   Heat the remaining olive oil in a large frying pan, add the aubergine strips and fry for about 10 minutes, turning frequently, until golden brown on all sides and tender. Drain on kitchen paper.

4   Bring a large saucepan of salted water to the boil. Add the pasta and cook in fast boiling water until *al dente* (tender but firm to the bite). Drain the pasta and toss with the tomato sauce and aubergine. Scatter with the basil leaves and serve, with plenty of grated Parmesan.

fast pasta sauces

Pasta is the quintessential fast food. Dried pasta cooks in just 10 minutes and can be combined with all manner of tasty sauces to create speedy dishes. It is an ideal choice for a quick supper when you return home from work, hungry and too tired to cook.

Look to the wonderful array of Italian ingredients in the supermarket to assemble mouthwatering pasta sauces in a matter of moments. Choose from soft cheeses that melt effortlessly, pots of ready-made pesto (red and green), dried chillies, preserved artichokes, sun-dried tomatoes, pancetta dice, and baby spinach and rocket leaves that wilt on contact with hot pasta. Select ripe, flavourful fresh tomatoes or use canned chopped tomatoes, and keep a wedge of Parmesan in the fridge, and some fresh herbs, such as parsley and basil.

Each of the following sauces is sufficient to serve 4; you will need to cook about 350g (12oz) dried pasta of your choice.

▲ **garlicky prawn and tomato sauce**
Peel 225g (8oz) raw tiger prawns. Heat 3 tbsp olive oil in a sauté pan. Add the prawns with 2 crushed garlic cloves and 1 deseeded and chopped fresh red chilli and sauté for 3–4 minutes or until the prawns turn pink. Add 8 deseeded and finely chopped plum tomatoes, along with 2 tbsp chopped flat leaf parsley and toss to mix. Immediately tip into bowls of freshly cooked hot pasta and serve.

tomato and chilli sauce

Cook 4 finely chopped garlic cloves in 2 tbsp olive oil until softened. Add 250g (9oz) baby plum tomatoes and 1–2 deseeded and chopped red chillies (depending on size, heat and palate). Cook over a gentle heat for about 15 minutes until the tomatoes soften and split. Mix in 2 tbsp each of torn basil leaves and chopped flat leaf parsley. Season with salt and pepper and toss with your favourite freshly cooked pasta.

three cheese sauce

Chop 125g (4oz) each of 3 creamy cheeses, such as ricotta, dolcelatte and Taleggio. Add to a pan of freshly cooked, hot tagliatelle or other pasta of your choice and toss until melted into an instant creamy sauce. Divide between warm bowls, scatter with about 4 tbsp chopped flat leaf parsley, plenty of freshly grated Parmesan and a generous grinding of black pepper. Serve straightaway.

▲ creamy chicken and mushroom sauce

Buy a large cooked chicken breast, remove the skin and chop the flesh into pieces. Sauté 125g (4oz) sliced button, oyster or chestnut mushrooms in 3 tbsp olive oil until softened. Add the chopped chicken, 150ml (¼ pint) dry white wine, 4 tbsp single cream, 2 tbsp finely chopped rosemary leaves, and salt and pepper. Cook, stirring occasionally, for 5 minutes, then serve with your favourite freshly cooked pasta.

pumpkin ravioli

These small, plump pasta circles are filled with pumpkin and crumbled amaretti biscuits, and served drizzled with a fragrant sage butter. The recipe is a speciality of Mantua, a beautiful city that boasts an impressive ducal palace with wonderful frescoes by Mantegna.

Illustrated on previous page

SERVES 6

FOR THE PASTA:
300g (11oz) Italian '00' plain flour
³/₄ teaspoon sea salt
3 large eggs

FOR THE STUFFING AND SAGE BUTTER:
1 small pumpkin, about 1kg (2¹/₄lb)
2 garlic cloves, peeled and crushed
6 amaretti biscuits, finely crumbled
100g (3¹/₂oz) Parmesan cheese, freshly grated
90g (3¹/₄oz) unsalted butter
handful of sage leaves
sea salt and freshly ground black pepper

1 Preheat the oven to 180°C (fan oven 160°C), gas mark 4. To make the stuffing, cut the pumpkin into large pieces using a sharp knife, and discard the seeds. Place the pumpkin on a foil-lined baking sheet and bake in the oven for 30 minutes. Allow to cool, then remove the skin. Put the pumpkin flesh into a food processor with the garlic and seasoning, and whiz to a purée. Mix the pumpkin purée with the crumbled amaretti and half of the Parmesan. Check the seasoning.

2 To make the pasta, heap the flour into a mound on a board and sprinkle over the salt. Make a well in the centre. Break the eggs into the well and gradually work them into the flour to form a dough. Knead until smooth and elastic.

3 Divide the pasta dough in half and roll out into two very thin sheets of equal size, using a pasta machine if possible. Place small mounds of the pumpkin mixture on one pasta sheet, spacing them about 5cm (2 inches) apart. Top with the second pasta sheet and press lightly around each mound of filling to seal. Cut out the ravioli, using a fluted 5cm (2 inch) round cutter.

4 Bring a large saucepan of salted water to the boil.   ρ in the ravioli and cook until *al dente* (tender but firm to the bite), about 2–3 minutes. Meanwhile, melt the butter in a small saucepan and add the sage leaves.

5 Drain the ravioli and divide between warm plates. Sprinkle with the remaining Parmesan and drizzle with the sage butter. Eat at once.

pansôti with walnut sauce

Triangles of fresh pasta are stuffed with a tasty mixture of fresh herbs, garlic and ricotta, and served with a creamy walnut sauce. This recipe is popular all along the Ligurian coastline and it takes its name, pansôti, from the regional name for ravioli. The walnut sauce can be made in advance, and is often referred to as 'winter pesto'.

SERVES 6

FOR THE PASTA:
250g (9oz) Italian '00' plain flour
1/2 teaspoon sea salt
2 medium eggs

FOR THE FILLING AND SAUCE:
60g (2 1/4oz) chopped chervil
60g (2 1/4oz) chopped chives
60g (2 1/4oz) chopped marjoram
2 garlic cloves
1 medium egg
90g (3 1/4oz) ricotta cheese
125g (4oz) slightly dry, coarse breadcrumbs, soaked in water and squeezed dry
125g (4oz) shelled walnuts
90g (3 1/4oz) Parmesan cheese, freshly grated
125ml (4fl oz) double cream
4 tablespoons extra virgin olive oil
sea salt and freshly ground black pepper

1   To make the pasta, heap the flour in a mound on a board, sprinkle over the salt and make a well in the centre. Break the eggs into the well and gradually work them into the flour, adding sufficient water to make a soft dough. Knead until smooth and elastic. Wrap in cling film and chill for 20 minutes.

2   For the filling, mix the chopped herbs, garlic, egg and ricotta together in a bowl and add half of the soaked breadcrumbs. Mix well, seasoning with salt and pepper to taste.

3   Blanch the walnuts in boiling water for 1 minute, then drain and peel off the skins. Place the nuts in a blender with the remaining soaked breadcrumbs, 1 tablespoon Parmesan, the cream and olive oil. Blend to a creamy consistency. Transfer the sauce to a small saucepan and warm gently.

4   Roll out the pasta dough, using a pasta machine, to the second thinnest setting. Cut into 6cm (2 1/2 inch) squares. Place a small amount of filling in the centre of each square and fold the dough back over to form a triangle, pressing the edges together lightly to seal in the filling.

5   Cook the pansôti in plenty of boiling salted water until *al dente* (tender but firm to the bite), about 3 minutes. Drain and serve topped with the walnut sauce and remaining Parmesan.

pasta with meatballs in tomato sauce

This is a classic dish from Campania, my home region. Minced beef, veal and pork are made into meatballs and cooked in a rich tomato sauce, to be served with pasta. Conveniently, both the sauce and meatballs can be made in advance.

SERVES 6

FOR THE MEATBALLS:
250g (9oz) lean beef mince
250g (9oz) lean veal mince
125g (4oz) lean pork mince
handful of flat leaf parsley, finely chopped
½ teaspoon oregano leaves, finely chopped
2 tablespoons dry vermouth
grated zest of 2 unwaxed lemons

100g (3½oz) soft, white breadcrumbs
2 large eggs
2 garlic cloves, peeled and crushed
sea salt and freshly ground black pepper

FOR THE SAUCE AND PASTA:
700g jar tomato passata
400g (14oz) penne, cellentani or macaroni

TO SERVE:
Parmesan cheese shavings

1   First, prepare the meatballs. Combine all the ingredients in a bowl and season generously with salt and pepper. Mix thoroughly with a wooden spoon until evenly blended. Shape into small balls, about 2cm (¾ inch) in diameter.

2   Pour the passata into a large shallow pan. Bring to a simmer and add the meatballs. Cover and cook over a medium heat for 40 minutes.

3   Towards the end of the cooking time, add the pasta to a large pan of boiling salted water and cook at a fast boil until al dente (tender but firm to the bite). Drain well.

4   Divide the hot pasta between warm bowls and pour the meatballs in tomato sauce over the top. Toss to mix, sprinkle with Parmesan shavings and serve at once.

spaghetti with Italian sausage

Enjoyed throughout the whole of Italy, but originating from the Marches, this is a great favourite with children. It is one of the easiest of the classic pasta dishes to prepare.

SERVES 6

350g (12oz) spaghetti
sea salt and freshly ground black pepper

FOR THE SAUCE:
750g (1lb 10oz) Italian sausage
2 tablespoons olive oil
1 onion, peeled and finely chopped
1 teaspoon oregano leaves
700g jar tomato passata
1 bay leaf
2 tablespoons dry vermouth

TO SERVE:
handful of flat leaf parsley, finely chopped

1 First prepare the sauce. Cut the sausage into 2.5cm (1 inch) pieces and place in a shallow pan with 6 tablespoons water. Bring to a simmer and cook until the water has evaporated.

2 Heat the olive oil in another pan, add the onion and sauté for about 5 minutes until soft, then add the sausage and oregano and cook for a further 5 minutes. Add the tomato passata, bay leaf and vermouth, and simmer uncovered for 30 minutes. Season with salt and pepper to taste.

3 Towards the end of the cooking time, add the spaghetti to a large pan of boiling salted water and cook at a fast boil until *al dente* (tender but firm to the bite), about 8–10 minutes. Drain well.

4 Divide the spaghetti between warm plates and pour the hot sauce over the top. Sprinkle with parsley and serve straightaway.

lasagne with chicken

Lasagne is always popular and it's an ideal dish for a family meal or informal party, not least because it can be made ahead of time. As a change from the familiar beef mince filling, this version – known as *lasagne alla cacciatore* in Italy – features chicken and mushrooms.

SERVES 6–8

250g packet egg lasagne (no pre-cook)

FOR THE FILLING:
6 chicken breasts
2 tablespoons olive oil
2 rosemary sprigs, leaves only, chopped
1 onion, peeled and finely chopped
175ml (6fl oz) white wine
2 x 400g cans chopped tomatoes
75g (3oz) unsalted butter
2 garlic cloves, peeled and crushed

500g (1lb 2oz) field mushrooms
handful of flat leaf parsley, finely chopped
handful of basil leaves, torn
sea salt and freshly ground black pepper

FOR THE SAUCE:
75g (3oz) unsalted butter
100g (3½oz) Italian '00' flour
600ml (1 pint) milk, warmed
50g (2oz) Parmesan cheese, freshly grated

TO SERVE (OPTIONAL):
extra Parmesan cheese, freshly grated

1 Preheat the oven to 200°C (fan oven 180°C), gas mark 6. For the filling, season the chicken breasts, rub with a little olive oil, place in a roasting tin and sprinkle with the rosemary. Roast for 20 minutes.

2 Meanwhile, heat the remaining olive oil in a saucepan, add the onion and cook for 5 minutes or until softened and golden. Add the wine and let it evaporate. Next add the chopped tomatoes and bring to a simmer. Season with salt and pepper, and simmer for 20 minutes.

3 In the meantime, heat the butter in a frying pan. Add the garlic and mushrooms and sauté until golden, turning once. Season with salt and pepper. Add the mushrooms to the tomatoes, along with the chopped parsley and basil.

4 Cut the cooked chicken breasts into strips and add to the mushroom and tomato mixture. Adjust the seasoning and set aside. Lower the oven setting to 180°C (fan oven 160°C), gas mark 4.

5 To make the sauce, melt the butter in a heavy-based pan, stir in the flour and cook for 1–2 minutes until golden. Add the warmed milk little by little to form a thick sauce, stirring over a medium heat until thick and smooth. Stir in half of the Parmesan and season to taste. (Unless you are assembling the dish straightaway, cover the surface with a damp piece of baking parchment to stop a skin forming.)

6 Line a lasagne dish with a layer of sauce, then cover with a layer of lasagne sheets. Spoon half of the chicken and mushroom mixture on top, then add another layer of lasagne. Cover with the remaining chicken and mushroom mixture and a final layer of lasagne.

7 Spread the rest of the sauce on top and sprinkle with the remaining Parmesan. Bake for 25 minutes until golden and bubbling. Serve with extra grated Parmesan if required.

polenta with wild mushrooms

Here a basic polenta is allowed to set, then cut into wedges, griddled and served topped with a wild mushroom sauce. It makes an elegant *primi piatti* (first course) for a special dinner.

SERVES 4

FOR THE POLENTA:
200g (7oz) coarse polenta
50g (2oz) unsalted butter, cut into cubes
50g (2oz) Parmesan cheese, freshly grated
sea salt and freshly ground black pepper

FOR THE MUSHROOM SAUCE:
700g (1½lb) wild or cultivated flat mushrooms
4 tablespoons olive oil
1 small garlic clove, peeled and crushed
1 tablespoon chopped thyme, plus sprigs to serve
150ml (¼ pint) white wine
2 tablespoons chopped flat leaf parsley

1 Bring 1.7 litres (3 pints) water to the boil in a large saucepan with 1 teaspoon salt added. Gradually add the polenta, letting it run through your fingers in a thin stream, and stirring constantly to prevent lumps. Simmer for 35 minutes, until the mixture comes away from the sides of the pan, stirring often.

2 When the polenta is cooked, stir in the butter, Parmesan and pepper to taste. (At this stage, you have what is known as 'wet polenta', which can be served as a simple accompaniment.)

3 While the polenta is still hot, spread it on to a dampened baking sheet or wooden board, to a 1cm (½ inch) thickness. Leave for about 1 hour until softly set.

4 Meanwhile, make the sauce. Halve or quarter any large mushrooms. Heat the olive oil and garlic in a pan, then add the mushrooms and thyme and cook over a high heat for 1 minute. Season with salt and pepper. Add the wine and boil vigorously until almost totally evaporated. Stir in the parsley.

5 Preheat a griddle pan or the grill. Cut the set polenta into triangles and griddle or grill on both sides until lightly charred. Serve on warm plates, topped with the mushroom sauce and a few thyme sprigs.

fried polenta sandwiches

Similar to the more familiar *mozzarella in carrozza*, this is a delicious way of using up leftover polenta. If you are unable to find fontina, you can use mozzarella cheese instead. A popular snack, with children and adults.

MAKES 6

FOR THE POLENTA:
600ml (1 pint) vegetable broth (page 47)
   or water
125g (4oz) coarse polenta
25g (1oz) Parmesan cheese, freshly grated
25g (1oz) unsalted butter
sea salt and freshly ground black pepper

TO ASSEMBLE AND COOK:
125g (4oz) fontina cheese
6 slices of prosciutto
plain flour, to dust
1 large egg, beaten
175g (6oz) fresh white breadcrumbs
olive oil, for shallow-frying

1   Pour the vegetable broth or water into a large saucepan, add ½ teaspoon salt and bring to the boil. Gradually add the polenta, letting it run through your fingers in a thin stream, and stirring constantly to prevent lumps forming. Simmer for 30 minutes, until the mixture comes away from the sides of the pan, stirring frequently.

2   When the polenta is cooked, stir in the Parmesan, butter and some pepper. Spread the hot polenta mixture on to a dampened baking sheet or wooden board, to a 1cm (½ inch) thickness. Leave for about 1 hour until set.

3   Cut the set polenta into rounds, using a 7.5cm (3 inch) cutter. Slice the fontina cheese to the same size as the polenta rounds. Sandwich a slice of cheese and a piece of prosciutto between two rounds of polenta. Press well together.

4   Dust the polenta sandwiches with flour to coat all over, then dip into the beaten egg, and finally into the breadcrumbs. Press lightly, so the breadcrumbs adhere.

5   Heat the olive oil in a large frying pan and shallow-fry the polenta sandwiches on both sides until golden brown. Drain on kitchen paper, then serve immediately.

rice balls

Enjoyed throughout Italy, these cheesy rice balls are known as *supplì di riso*, or *supplì al telefono* because the mozzarella stretches like telephone wires as they are eaten. Ideal party food or antipasto, they are a good way of using leftover risotto, though here the risotto is freshly made.

SERVES 4

800ml (1 pint 7fl oz) vegetable broth (page 47)
50g (2oz) unsalted butter
275g (10oz) risotto rice (such as vialone nano, carnaroli or arborio)
175g (6oz) mozzarella cheese, cut into small cubes
6 shallots, peeled and finely chopped
finely grated zest of 1 large unwaxed orange

handful of mixed herbs (such as flat leaf parsley, basil and oregano), chopped
6 tablespoons freshly grated Parmesan cheese
sea salt and freshly ground black pepper

TO ASSEMBLE AND COOK:
1 egg, lightly beaten
50g (2oz) fresh white breadcrumbs
6 tablespoons olive oil

1 Heat the broth in a saucepan until almost boiling, then reduce the heat and keep at a low simmer.

2 Heat the butter in a wide, heavy-based saucepan. Add the rice and stir, using a wooden spoon, until the grains are well coated and glistening, about 1 minute. Add a ladleful of hot stock and simmer, stirring, until it has been absorbed. Continue to add the stock at intervals and cook as before, until all the liquid has been absorbed and the rice is *al dente* (tender but retaining a bite), about 18–20 minutes.

3 Add the mozzarella, shallots, orange zest, mixed herbs, Parmesan, and salt and pepper to taste. Mix well. Remove from the heat and let cool. (The rice is easier to handle and shape when it is cold.)

4 Using your hands, shape the rice mixture into 8 balls. Dip each one into the beaten egg and coat well, then roll in the breadcrumbs to coat. Use your fingers to press crumbs on to any uncoated surface.

5 Heat the olive oil in a frying pan. Fry the rice balls, in batches if necessary, until golden on all sides, about 8 minutes. Drain well on kitchen paper. Serve hot or cold.

saffron risotto

This classic *risotto alla milanese*, is a speciality of Lombardy. I use saffron threads rather than the powdered form, which tends to be of a lesser quality and flavour. My sisters often make this dish as their children adore it – they call it 'happy food' because of its bright yellow colour.

SERVES 4

900ml (1½ pints) vegetable broth (page 47)
50g (2oz) unsalted butter
1 tablespoon olive oil
8 shallots, peeled and finely chopped
½ teaspoon saffron threads
275g (10oz) risotto rice (such as vialone nano, carnaroli or arborio)

about 75ml (2½fl oz) white wine
100g (3½oz) Parmesan cheese, freshly grated, plus extra to serve
2 tablespoons single cream
handful of flat leaf parsley, coarsely chopped (optional)
sea salt and freshly ground black pepper

1   Heat the broth in a saucepan until almost boiling, then reduce the heat and keep at a low simmer.

2   Heat the butter and olive oil in a wide, heavy-based saucepan over a medium heat. Add the shallots and cook for 1–2 minutes, until softened but not browned. Add the saffron and stir until its yellow colour is released, then add the rice. Stir with a wooden spoon until the rice grains are well coated and glistening, about 1 minute.

3   Add the wine and stir until absorbed. Add a ladleful of hot stock and simmer, stirring until it has been absorbed. Continue to add the stock at intervals and cook as before, until the liquid is absorbed and the rice is *al dente* (tender but retaining a bite), about 18–20 minutes. Save the last ladleful of stock.

4   Add the Parmesan, cream, reserved stock, chopped parsley if using, and some salt and pepper. Stir well, then remove from the heat, cover and leave to rest for 2 minutes. Spoon into warm bowls and serve with extra Parmesan.

tomato risotto

The simplicity of this dish appeals to me and probably accounts for its popularity with children as well as grown-ups. It's almost impossible to imagine Italian food without tomatoes. Use a full-flavoured variety – firm, red and with a good fruity scent.

SERVES 4

900ml (1½ pints) vegetable broth (page 47)

50g (2oz) unsalted butter

1 tablespoon olive oil

8 shallots, peeled and finely chopped

2 garlic cloves, peeled and crushed

275g (10oz) risotto rice (such as vialone nano, carnaroli or arborio)

about 75ml (2½fl oz) white wine

8 firm, ripe tomatoes, deseeded and coarsely chopped

100g (3½oz) Parmesan cheese, freshly grated

large handful of basil leaves, torn

sea salt and freshly ground black pepper

TO SERVE (OPTIONAL):

freshly grated Parmesan cheese

handful of basil leaves, torn

1 Put the vegetable broth into a saucepan. Heat until almost boiling, then reduce the heat until barely simmering to keep it hot.

2 Heat the butter and olive oil in a wide, heavy-based saucepan over a medium heat. Add the shallots and cook for 1–2 minutes, until softened but not browned. Add the garlic and mix well.

3 Add the rice and stir, using a wooden spoon, until the grains are well coated and glistening, about 1 minute. Pour in the wine and stir until it has been completely absorbed.

4 Add a ladleful of hot broth and simmer, stirring, until it has been absorbed. Continue to add the stock in this way then, after 10 minutes, add the tomatoes. Add the rest of the stock at intervals and cook as before, for a further 8–10 minutes, until the liquid has been absorbed and the rice is *al dente* (tender but retaining a bite). Reserve the last ladleful of stock.

5 Stir in the Parmesan, reserved stock, basil, salt and pepper. Remove from the heat, cover and rest for 2 minutes. Spoon into warm bowls, sprinkle with grated Parmesan and basil if using, and serve.

risotto with asparagus, peas and basil

One of my all-time favourite risottos. So light, fresh and vibrantly green, it reminds me of early summer, when asparagus and peas grow in abundance. Do make the most of vegetables when they are in season, to enjoy them at their finest and sweetest.

SERVES 4

900ml (1¹/₂ pints) vegetable broth (page 47)
50g (2oz) unsalted butter
1 tablespoon olive oil
8 shallots, peeled and finely chopped
275g (10oz) risotto rice (such as vialone nano, carnaroli or arborio)
about 75ml (2¹/₂fl oz) white wine
150g (5oz) podded fresh or frozen peas (thawed)

350g (12oz) asparagus spears, cut into 4cm (1¹/₂ inch) lengths
finely grated zest of 1 unwaxed lemon
100g (3¹/₂oz) Parmesan cheese, freshly grated
large handful of basil leaves, torn
sea salt and freshly ground black pepper
TO SERVE (OPTIONAL):
handful of basil leaves, torn
freshly grated Parmesan cheese

1 Put the vegetable broth into a saucepan. Heat until almost boiling, then reduce the heat until barely simmering to keep it hot.

2 Heat the butter and olive oil in a wide, heavy-based saucepan over a medium heat. Add the shallots and cook for 1–2 minutes, until softened but not browned.

3 Add the rice and stir, using a wooden spoon, until the grains are well coated and glistening, about 1 minute. Pour in the wine and stir until completely absorbed.

4 Add a ladleful of hot stock and simmer, stirring, until it has been absorbed. Continue to add the stock in this way then, after 10 minutes, add the fresh peas if using, asparagus and lemon zest and mix well. Continue to add the stock at intervals and cook as before, for a further 8–10 minutes, until the liquid has been absorbed and the rice is *al dente* (tender but retaining a bite). If using frozen peas, add 2 minutes before the end of cooking. Reserve the last ladleful of stock.

5 Add the Parmesan, reserved stock, basil, salt and pepper. Mix well. Remove from the heat, cover and leave to rest for 2 minutes. Spoon into warm bowls and top with more basil and grated Parmesan if using. Serve immediately.

5 fish and shellfish

prawns and white beans Venetian style

The Venetians love seafood and always cook it very carefully. The combination of prawns and beans in this delicate salad is delicious, and the textures are diverse. It is a simple recipe – just remember to put the cannellini beans to soak the evening before.

SERVES 4

125g (4oz) dried cannellini beans, soaked in
  cold water overnight
2 rosemary sprigs
3 bay leaves
3 thyme sprigs
3 flat leaf parsley sprigs
4 garlic cloves, unpeeled
500g (1lb) large raw prawns in shell
2 celery stalks, finely chopped
juice of 1 lemon
handful of flat leaf parsley, chopped
2–3 tablespoons extra virgin olive oil
sea salt and freshly ground black pepper
lemon wedges, to serve

1 Drain the cannellini beans and place in a large pan. Add plenty of cold water to cover, and the herbs and unpeeled garlic. Bring to the boil, then reduce the heat and cook for about 1½ hours or until the beans are tender. Drain the beans and discard the herbs and garlic.

2 Add the prawns to a pan of boiling salted water and simmer for 2 minutes or until they just turn pink. Immediately drain, peel and devein them.

3 Combine the beans and prawns in a bowl and add the celery, along with the lemon juice and parsley. Season well with salt and pepper, drizzle with the extra virgin olive oil and toss to mix. Serve with lemon wedges.

fritto misto

This dish of mixed fried fish is very popular throughout Italy. In my native Campania, it is usually made of tiny squid, cuttlefish rings and scampi, dusted with flour before being deep-fried in olive oil. It is served crisp and piping hot, with lemon wedges.

SERVES 6

300g (11oz) squid

300g (11oz) scampi tails or large raw prawns
  in shell

300g (11oz) monkfish fillet, skinned

125g (4oz) Italian '00' flour, to coat

oil, for deep-frying

sea salt

lemon wedges, to serve

1 To clean whole squid, pull the pouch and tentacles apart and remove the transparent quill from the pouch. Cut the tentacles away from the head just below the eyes and discard the head, reserving the tentacles. Peel off the transparent outer skin covering the pouch, then cut into rings. Baby squid can simply be halved.

2 Peel away the shell from the prawns, leaving the tail end intact if you like. Prise out the dark intestinal vein that runs down the back.

3 Cut the monkfish into cubes. Wash all the seafood and dry it well on kitchen paper. Scatter the flour on a board or tray and toss the seafood in it to coat each piece thoroughly.

4 Heat the oil in a deep-fat fryer or deep heavy-based saucepan to 190°C, or until a cube of bread dropped in browns in 30 seconds. Deep-fry the seafood, a few pieces at a time, until golden and cooked through, about 2–3 minutes.

5 Drain on kitchen paper, sprinkle with salt and serve at once accompanied by lemon wedges.

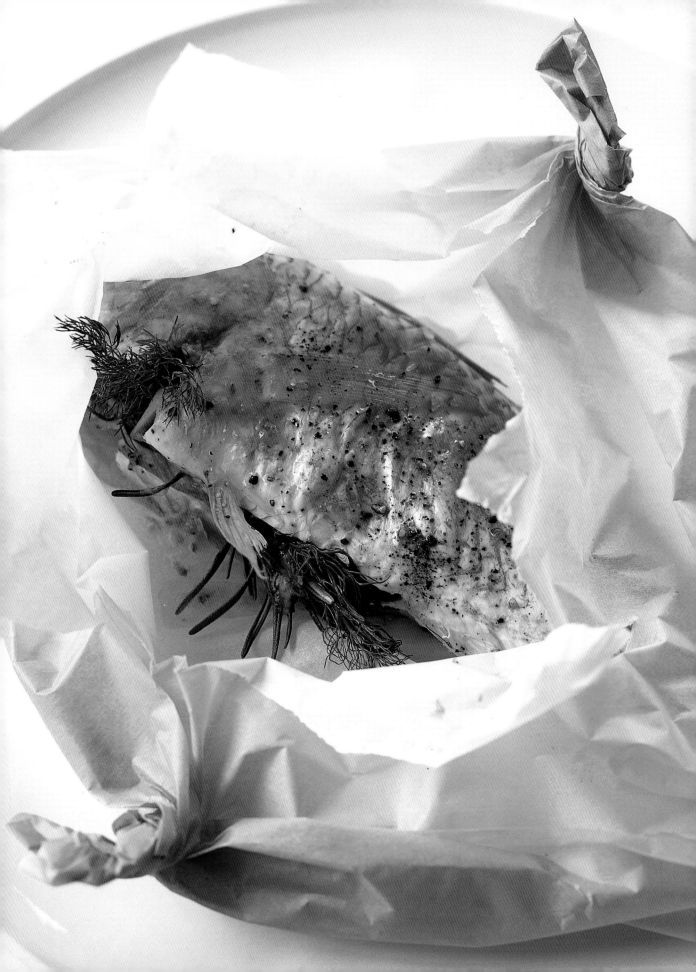

red mullet in an envelope

Baking red mullet in sealed parchment parcels is an excellent way of retaining their delicate flavour and enticing aroma as they cook. The flavour is further enhanced by topping the fish with a piquant anchovy butter before baking. Ask your fishmonger to clean the fish, leaving the liver in if possible, as this adds to the flavour.

Illustrated on previous page

SERVES 4

4 red mullet, each about 200g (7oz), cleaned
4 fennel frond sprigs
large handful of basil leaves
large handful of rosemary leaves
2 tablespoons olive oil
sea salt and freshly ground black pepper

FOR THE ANCHOVY BUTTER:
125g (4oz) unsalted butter, softened
6–8 anchovy fillets in oil, drained

1 Preheat the oven to 220°C (fan oven 200°C), gas mark 7. For the anchovy butter, put the softened butter into a bowl, add the anchovy fillets and mash together, using a fork. Chill until ready to use.

2 Rinse and dry the fish well, and put some of the herbs into each cavity. Cut 4 large rectangles of baking parchment (large enough to envelop the fish). Brush the red mullet with olive oil, then place a fish in the centre of each parchment rectangle.

3 Sprinkle more herbs on top of the fish and season with salt and pepper. Bring the long edges of the paper up over the fish and fold together firmly. Twist the ends of the paper to seal. Place the parcels on a baking tray and bake in the oven for 15–20 minutes.

4 Serve the fish in their fragrant parcels, to be opened at the table.

trout with parsley and lemon cream sauce

Trout are to be found in abundance in the rivers of the mountainous Trentino area in the north, which borders Austria. This freshwater fish is best cooked soon after purchase in a light broth. Here it is served with a lemon and parsley cream sauce.

SERVES 4

4 trout, each about 225g (8oz), cleaned
1.2 litres (2 pints) fish broth (page 46) or
  vegetable broth (page 47)
sea salt and freshly ground black pepper

FOR THE SAUCE:
50g (2oz) unsalted butter
250ml (8fl oz) double cream
juice of 2 lemons

TO SERVE:
handful of flat leaf parsley, finely chopped

1 Rinse the trout inside and out. Bring the fish or vegetable broth to the boil in a wide, shallow pan. Place the trout in the broth and poach gently just until the flesh is opaque and the eyes are white, about 10 minutes. Lift out and drain well.

2 Meanwhile, make the sauce. Melt the butter in a small saucepan, then add the cream, lemon juice and some salt. Bring to a simmer, stirring constantly, and simmer for about 5 minutes until reduced. Taste and adjust the seasoning.

3 Place the trout on warm plates. Pour the sauce over the fish, then scatter generously with chopped parsley and serve at once.

stuffed sardines

Sardines are stuffed in many different ways all around the Italian coast. The rosemary and garlic in this dish identify it as Venetian. It takes a little while to prepare sardines for stuffing, but the technique is really not difficult.

SERVES 4

800g (1³/₄lb) fresh sardines, cleaned

5 tablespoons white breadcrumbs (slightly dry)

1 tablespoon chopped rosemary leaves, plus an
   extra stem

2 tablespoons chopped flat leaf parsley

2 garlic cloves, peeled and finely chopped

6 tablespoons olive oil

juice of 2 lemons

sea salt and freshly ground black pepper

1 Preheat the oven to 200°C (fan oven 180°C), gas mark 6. Cut off the heads from the sardines. Slit down the underside, open out the fish and place flesh-side down on a board. Press down along the spine to flatten and loosen the backbone, then turn over and remove the bone. Wash the fish and pat dry thoroughly.

2 For the stuffing, put the breadcrumbs, rosemary, parsley, garlic and some salt and pepper into a bowl. Pour in 4 tablespoons of the olive oil and mix thoroughly.

3 With the open sardines skin-side down, divide the stuffing between them, spreading it along the middle of each fish. Fold the sides together, so the sardines resume their original shape.

4 Place the sardines, side by side, in a lightly oiled roasting tray in which they fit snugly in a single layer. Sprinkle with salt and pepper. Drizzle with the remaining olive oil and the lemon juice, and lay the rosemary stem on top (for extra flavour). Bake for about 15 minutes until the fish are cooked and a little crispy on top. Serve warm.

marinated fish

Fish is highly valued in Italy, and it is eaten regularly – not surprisingly, considering the extensive 1500 miles of Italian coastline. Every region has its own special fish dishes, from the fritto misto and fish soups of Calabria in the south, to the marinated fish dishes typical of middle Italy and seafood dishes of Veneto in the north west.

Fish cooks quickly, and in Italy it is cooked very simply. Whole fish, steaks and fillets generally benefit from marinating first, especially if they are to be griddled, grilled, barbecued or roasted in the oven. An oil-based marinade helps to prevent tender fish from becoming dry during cooking. Olive oil is the usual basis, with additional flavourings to suit the particular fish – perhaps a hint of lemon juice and/or zest, balsamic vinegar, a pinch of chilli, finely chopped shallots, and a handful of finely chopped herbs. Try the following recipes, varying the flavourings to taste.

▲ swordfish steaks with capers and anchovies

To serve 4, place 4 swordfish steaks, each about 225g (8oz), in a dish in a single layer. Mix 6 tbsp olive oil with 3 tbsp dry white wine, 2 finely chopped shallots, 1 tbsp rinsed small capers, 4 drained, chopped anchovies in oil and the juice of 1 lemon. Leave to marinate for 1 hour, then remove. Grill or barbecue for 6 minutes on each side, depending on thickness, basting occasionally with the marinade.

monkfish spiedini

To serve 4, ask the fishmonger to fillet and skin 1kg (2¼lb) monkfish tail. Cut into 2.5cm (1 inch) cubes. Mix the juice of 2 lemons with 2 finely chopped garlic cloves, 1 deseeded and chopped red chilli, 1–2 tsp finely chopped rosemary leaves and 4 tbsp olive oil. Pour over the fish and marinate for 1 hour. Thread the monkfish on to 4 or 8 skewers. Grill for a maximum of 6 minutes, turning once.

grilled, marinated sardines

For an antipasto to serve 4, clean and remove the heads from 8 sardines. Place in a dish. Mix 6 tbsp olive oil with 2 tbsp white wine vinegar, 2 crushed garlic cloves, 1 deseeded and chopped red chilli and 2 tbsp finely chopped parsley. Pour over the sardines and leave to marinate for 1 hour, turning once. Remove the sardines from the marinade and grill or barbecue for 12 minutes, turning once and basting occasionally with the marinade.

▲ sea bass fillets with lemon and chilli

To serve 4, place 4 sea bass fillets, each about 200g (7oz), skin-side down in a shallow ovenproof dish. In a bowl, combine the finely grated zest and juice of 2 lemons, 4 tbsp olive oil, 1 deseeded and finely chopped red chilli, 1 finely chopped garlic clove and a finely sliced red onion. Pour over the fish, cover and marinate in a cool place for 1 hour. Season the fish and bake at 200°C, gas 6 for 15 minutes or until just tender. Serve at once.

whole fish baked in tomato sauce

Baking a whole fish in a sauce of onions, wine, tomato and celery is an excellent way of keeping the fish succulent, while imparting extra flavour at the same time. You can use any suitable sized whole white fish. Try, for instance, sea bass, grey mullet, hake or haddock. Ask your fishmonger to bone the fish, keeping it whole.

SERVES 4

1 sea bream, about 1.4kg (3lb), or other whole
  white fish, cleaned and boned out
1–2 tablespoons olive oil
sea salt and freshly ground black pepper

FOR THE SAUCE:
4 tablespoons olive oil
1 medium onion, peeled and finely chopped
1 small celery stalk, finely chopped
1 garlic clove, peeled and finely chopped
1 tablespoon chopped flat leaf parsley
8 tomatoes, skinned and coarsely chopped
150ml (¼ pint) dry white wine

1 Preheat the oven to 200°C (fan oven 180°C), gas mark 6. Wash and pat the fish dry, then season with salt inside and out. Place in an oiled roasting tin and brush the skin with olive oil.

2 For the sauce, heat the olive oil in a pan, add the onion, celery, garlic and parsley, and sauté until the vegetables are soft. Add the tomatoes and wine and cook for 10 minutes. Season with salt and pepper to taste.

3 Spoon the sauce over and around the fish. Cover the tin with foil and bake in the oven for about 30 minutes until the fish is cooked. To test, insert a knife into the thickest part of the body and lift out a little of the flesh – it should be opaque but still moist.

4 Carefully transfer the fish to a warm serving platter and spoon the sauce around. Serve at once.

stuffed sole in saffron sauce

Saffron has always been a feature of Venetian cooking. In times past, this exotic spice was viewed as a sign of wealth, as it gave food the coveted colour of real gold. It has a distinctive, complex flavour and must be measured accurately – too much could truly ruin a dish. Get your fishmonger to fillet the fish and remember to ask for the bones – to make the broth.

SERVES 6

3 Dover soles, filleted
2 tablespoons sultanas
125g (4oz) young, tender spinach leaves,
  stalks removed
2 tablespoons pine nuts
2 shallots, peeled and very finely chopped
600ml (1 pint) fish broth (page 46)
20 saffron threads
125ml (4fl oz) dry white wine
40g (1¹/₂oz) unsalted butter, cut into small
  pieces
sea salt and freshly ground black pepper

1 Rinse the sole fillets and pat dry. Put the sultanas into a bowl, add 3–4 tablespoons hot water and leave for 10 minutes to plump up. Drain and pat dry with kitchen paper.

2 Season the sole fillets with salt and pepper on both sides. Lay the spinach leaves overlapping on each fillet and place some sultanas, pine nuts and chopped shallot on top. Roll up the fillets and secure them with string or wooden cocktail sticks.

3 Bring the fish broth to the boil in a wide, shallow pan. Turn the heat down, then add the fish bundles and cover the pan. Poach gently, with the liquid barely simmering, for 6 minutes.

4 Meanwhile put the saffron threads into a small mortar and pound with the pestle until crushed. Add a tablespoon or two of the hot fish liquid to dissolve the mixture.

5 Using a slotted spoon, remove the sole bundles from the fish broth and place on a w. m plate; keep hot. Pour off half of the broth. Add the saffron mixture and wine to the remaining broth in the pan and boil to reduce by half over a high heat. Stir in the pieces of butter, a few at a time.

6 When all the butter has been incorporated, taste and adjust the seasoning. Spoon the sauce around the sole bundles and serve.

roasted monkfish with garlic

Monkfish has a meaty texture and its flavour is exquisite, but it is quite expensive. This is an impressive dish for a dinner party, best served with a simple accompaniment, such as grilled tomatoes. If you're not keen on fennel seeds, simply omit them. Ask your fishmonger to skin and fillet the monkfish by removing the central bone to give two meaty fillets.

SERVES 4

1kg (2¼ lb) monkfish tail, filleted and skinned
1 large garlic bulb, as fresh as possible
4–5 bay leaves
50ml (2 fl oz) olive oil
1 teaspoon thyme leaves
½ teaspoon fennel seeds (optional)
juice of 1 lemon
sea salt and freshly ground black pepper

1 Preheat the oven to 200°C (fan oven 180°C), gas mark 6. Remove all traces of the thin, grey membrane covering the monkfish, then rinse and dry the fish. To hold the fillets together, tie a length of string around the length of the fish, then secure with string at intervals (as shown).

2 Peel 2 garlic cloves from the bulb and cut them into thin slices. Make some incisions in the fish and push in the garlic slices. Tuck the bay leaves under the string.

3 Preheat a baking tray in the oven for a few minutes. Add half of the olive oil, then lay the fish on the hot tray and turn carefully to coat with the hot oil. Season with salt and pepper, and scatter with the thyme leaves and fennel seeds if using. Drizzle the lemon juice and remaining olive oil over the fish and surround with the rest of the unpeeled garlic cloves.

4 Roast in the oven for 20–30 minutes, basting frequently. Serve with grilled tomatoes if you like.

tuna steaks with capers

Fine quality swordfish and tuna are caught off the Sicilian coast and this is a speciality of the island. The fish steaks are marinated in white wine with rosemary and garlic, then grilled and served with a sauce of capers and lemon – both found in abundance in Sicily.

SERVES 4

4 tuna or swordfish steaks, each about
    225g (8oz)
250ml (8fl oz) dry white wine
1 rosemary sprig, finely chopped
4 garlic cloves, peeled and finely chopped
olive oil, to brush
2 tablespoons day-old white breadcrumbs,
    lightly toasted
sea salt and freshly ground black pepper

FOR THE DRESSING:

4 tablespoons extra virgin olive oil
finely grated zest and juice of 1 unwaxed lemon
1 tablespoon salted capers, soaked in cold water
    for 20 minutes and drained

1 Place the fish steaks in a shallow dish and season with salt and pepper. Add the wine, rosemary and garlic, and turn the steaks to coat all over. Leave to marinate for at least an hour.

2 Drain the fish and pat dry, reserving the marinade. Heat a ridged cast-iron griddle pan, or preheat the grill to high and brush the griddle (or grill) pan with olive oil. Cook the fish steaks for about 6–8 minutes on each side depending on thickness, basting frequently with the reserved marinade.

3 Meanwhile, make the dressing. In a small bowl, whisk the olive oil with the lemon juice and zest, capers, and some salt and pepper.

4 Sprinkle the cooked tuna or swordfish with the toasted breadcrumbs. Place on warm plates and drizzle with the dressing. Serve with a mixed leaf salad.

tuna and spinach pie

This is another northern speciality from Liguria, using a wonderfully complementary combination of tuna and anchovy with spinach and potatoes. Baked in a cake tin, it makes a good family dish – real Italian comfort food!

SERVES 4

300g (11oz) medium old potatoes (Desirée, Pentland Crown, King Edward)

5 tablespoons olive oil, plus extra to brush

fine dried breadcrumbs, to coat tin

1kg (2¼lb) spinach, tough stalks removed

1 onion, peeled and finely chopped

1 garlic clove, peeled and very finely chopped

handful of flat leaf parsley, chopped

generous grating of nutmeg

2 eggs, plus 1 egg yolk

6 tablespoons freshly grated Parmesan cheese

125g (4oz) canned tuna or bottled tuna in best quality olive oil

2 anchovy fillets, chopped

sea salt and freshly ground black pepper

1 Cook the potatoes in their skins in boiling salted water until soft, about 20 minutes. Drain and peel. Mash the potatoes smoothly, using a potato ricer, or food processor fitted with a fine grating disc, or by hand. Add 2 tablespoons of the olive oil to the potato purée and mix well.

2 Preheat the oven to 190°C (fan oven 170°C), gas mark 5. Line an 18cm (7 inch) spring-release cake tin with greaseproof paper or baking parchment, then brush with a little olive oil. Sprinkle the base and sides with breadcrumbs to coat, then carefully shake out any excess.

3 Wash the spinach well and place in a large pan with only the water that clings to the leaves after washing and 1 teaspoon salt. Cook over a medium high heat until wilted and tender. Drain thoroughly and, as soon as it is cool enough to handle, squeeze out as much moisture as possible using your hands. Chop the spinach coarsely.

4 Heat 3 tablespoons olive oil in a sauté pan, add the onion and cook gently for 5 minutes. Now add the garlic and parsley, then mix in the spinach and nutmeg, turning it over frequently. Add the contents of the pan to the potato purée.

5 Add the eggs, egg yolk, Parmesan and some pepper, then flake the tuna into the mixture and add the anchovy fillets. Mix well, then taste and adjust the seasoning.

6 Spoon the tuna and potato mixture into the prepared tin and bake in the oven for 40 minutes. Serve warm or at room temperature.

stuffed braised squid

This is a speciality of Puglia. Cleaned whole squid are stuffed, then braised on a bed of vegetables and potatoes, for a rustic, comforting dish that looks so tempting. During cooking the potatoes take on the flavours of the fish juices to delicious effect. Use fresh rather than frozen fish, if possible.

SERVES 4–6

12 medium squid, 10–12cm (4–5 inches) long, cleaned and tentacles reserved (see page 108)
3 tablespoons olive oil, plus extra to oil dish
1 onion, peeled and sliced
1 garlic clove, unpeeled
2 large plum tomatoes, skinned, deseeded and coarsely chopped
1 tablespoon chopped flat leaf parsley
450g (1lb) old potatoes (King Edward, Desirée, Pentland Crown)
1 small hot red chilli, deseeded and chopped
40g (1½oz) pecorino cheese, grated
sea salt and freshly ground black pepper
flat leaf parsley sprigs, to serve

FOR THE STUFFING:

150g (5oz) dry, firm-textured bread, torn into small pieces
1 medium egg, lightly beaten
1 garlic clove, peeled and finely chopped
1 tablespoon chopped flat leaf parsley
finely grated zest of 1 unwaxed lemon

1 First make the stuffing. Put the bread into a small bowl, add just enough warm water to cover and leave to soak for 5 minutes. Drain and squeeze dry. Mix the bread with the rest of the stuffing ingredients, and season with salt and pepper.

2 Spoon the stuffing into the squid pouches, only half filling them to allow room for expansion during cooking. Seal the open end of the squid pouches with wooden cocktail sticks.

3 Preheat the oven to 180°C (fan oven 160°C), gas mark 4 (unless you prefer to cook the dish on the hob). Lightly oil a 3 litre (5 pint) round casserole (flameproof if cooking on the hob). Scatter the onion, garlic, tomatoes, parsley and 3 tablespoons water in the dish and season with salt and pepper.

4 Peel the potatoes and cut into 1cm (½ inch) thick slices. Arrange slightly overlapping on top of the onion and tomato mixture and sprinkle with the chilli and more salt and pepper. Arrange the stuffed squid pouches and tentacles on top. Sprinkle with the cheese and drizzle with 3 tablespoons olive oil.

5 Cover and cook in the oven for about 45 minutes, or simmer slowly over a low heat on the hob for 1 hour until the squid and potatoes are tender. Check the casserole occasionally to be sure it remains at a slow simmer. Scatter with parsley and serve.

6 poultry and meat

braised lemon chicken

A light, lemony flavoured chicken casserole, which needs nothing else with it, apart from some crusty bread to mop up the juices, and perhaps a leafy salad. You must use a good chicken though, or you could use chicken pieces – meaty thighs would be ideal.

SERVES 4

1 free-range chicken, about 1.5kg (3¼lb), cut into 8 pieces
2–3 tablespoons plain flour, to dust
3 tablespoons olive oil

thinly pared zest of 3 lemons, finely chopped
1 small onion, peeled and finely chopped
2 sage sprigs, leaves only, chopped
350ml (12 fl oz) dry white wine
sea salt and freshly ground black pepper

1 Pat the chicken pieces dry with kitchen paper, then dust with flour to coat lightly all over.

2 Heat the olive oil in a large, heavy sauté pan over a medium high heat. Add the chicken pieces to the pan, and brown well on all sides. Using a slotted spoon, transfer the chicken to a plate and season with salt and pepper to taste.

3 Reduce the heat to medium low and add the lemon zest, onion and sage to the oil remaining in the pan. Sauté until the onion is golden and tender, about 10 minutes.

4 Return the chicken to the pan, along with the juices that have accumulated on the plate. Pour the wine over the chicken, partially cover the pan and simmer gently for 50–55 minutes or until the chicken is very tender and most of the wine has evaporated. The chicken should be nutty brown in colour and glazed with the pan juices. Check the seasoning.

5 Arrange the chicken pieces on warm plates. Skim the fat from the pan juices, taste and adjust the seasoning. If too thick, stir in 1–2 tablespoons water. Pour the juices over the chicken and serve.

chicken with tomato and rosemary sauce

Known as *pollo in potacchio*, this dish has the aromas of the Marche region – garlic, chilli and lemon zest, allied with abundant rosemary. *Potacchio* describes a sauce that is added to chicken or rabbit for its final cooking. Just like any other herb, rosemary is sweeter in the spring with its new shoots, and gets stronger later in the year when you'll need to use it with discretion.

SERVES 4–6

1 free-range chicken, about 1.5kg (3¼lb), cut
  into about 8 pieces
1 unwaxed lemon, halved
2 tablespoons olive oil
50g (2oz) unsalted butter
150ml (¼ pint) dry white wine
1 onion, peeled and finely chopped
1 garlic clove, peeled and finely chopped
sea salt and freshly ground black pepper

FOR THE SAUCE:

3 shallots or 1 small onion, peeled
leaves from 2–3 rosemary sprigs
coarsely grated zest of 1 unwaxed lemon
½ dried red chilli
3 tablespoons olive oil
400g (14oz) can chopped tomatoes

TO SERVE:
few small rosemary sprigs

1   Wash the chicken pieces and pat dry with kitchen paper. Rub them with the lemon halves, squeezing out the juice as you do so.

2   Heat the olive oil and butter in a large sauté pan. When the butter begins to foam, add the chicken pieces and fry on all sides until golden brown. Add the white wine, bring to the boil and let bubble for 1 minute. Turn the heat down and add the onion. Cook for a few minutes to soften, then add the garlic and some salt and pepper. Cook for 20 minutes, turning the chicken from time to time.

3   While the chicken is cooking, prepare the sauce. Chop the shallots or onion, rosemary leaves, lemon zest and chilli very finely together. Heat the olive oil in a frying pan and, when hot, add the finely chopped ingredients. Sauté very gently for 5 minutes or so, then add the chopped tomatoes and some salt. Cook for 15 minutes, stirring frequently.

4   Now that the sauce is cooked, add it to the chicken, and stir to mix in the cooking juices at the bottom of the sauté pan. Leave over a gentle heat for another 15 minutes, to allow the chicken to absorb the flavours of the sauce. Taste and adjust the seasoning, then serve scattered with rosemary.

chicken breasts with a vegetable relish

Chicken breasts are baked with onions and sage, then served with a *caponata* style relish – an aubergine stew with celery and yellow pepper, which is slightly *agro dolce* (sweet and sour). This *caponata* is Sardinian, but you can vary the vegetables – mushrooms would be a good inclusion.

SERVES 4

4 chicken breast fillets (with skin), each
  about 150g (5oz)
1 tablespoon chopped sage
2 tablespoons olive oil
900g (2lb) onions, peeled and very
  finely sliced
sea salt and freshly ground black pepper

FOR THE VEGETABLE RELISH:

1 yellow pepper, about 150g (5oz)
125g (4oz) aubergine
100g (3½oz) celery
200ml (7fl oz) red wine vinegar
4 tablespoons olive oil
1 tablespoon tomato purée
1 tablespoon caster sugar

1 Preheat the oven to 200°C (fan oven 180°C), gas mark 6. Rub the chicken breasts all over with salt, pepper and chopped sage. Use half of the olive oil to grease a small roasting tin or shallow baking dish.

2 For the relish, cut the vegetables into small pieces, each about 1cm (½ inch). Put them into a saucepan with the wine vinegar and pour in 200ml (7fl oz) water; the liquid should be level with the vegetables. Add 1 teaspoon salt. Bring to the boil, lower the heat and simmer for 10 minutes.

3 Meanwhile, lay the seasoned chicken breasts in the dish and scatter the onions on top. Sprinkle with salt and pepper and pour over the remaining olive oil. Bake for 20 minutes or until the chicken is tender and cooked through. To test, pierce the thickest part with the tip of a knife; the juices should run clear (not at all pink). The onion should be just tender, crisp on the top and juicy underneath.

4 In the meantime, drain the relish vegetables. Heat the olive oil in a frying pan and stir in the tomato purée and sugar. Cook for 2 minutes, to caramelise the sugar. Now add the vegetables and turn to coat them in the caramelised sugar and oil mixture. Turn the heat down and cook for a further 15 minutes, stirring frequently. The vegetables should be just crisp. Season with salt and pepper.

5 Spoon the vegetable relish on to warm plates and top with the baked chicken breasts to serve.

pheasant with olives

Pheasant is cooked during the Italian hunting season, which runs from September through to March. It is usually hung for a couple of days – rather less than the typical 5 or 6 days in this country. Here I have roasted the pheasant simply with olives, juniper berries, fennel seeds and pancetta. This is how I imagine the *cacciatore*, or hunters, might cook their booty in their little stoves in the middle of the forest.

SERVES 2

1 oven-ready pheasant
50g (2oz) pancetta or rindless streaky bacon,
  sliced
125g (4oz) pitted black olives
1 tablespoon fennel seeds
15g (¹/₂oz) unsalted butter
2 tablespoons olive oil
1 tablespoon juniper berries, crushed
125ml (4 fl oz) dry white wine
50ml (2 fl oz) chicken broth (page 47)
sea salt and freshly ground black pepper

1 Preheat the oven to 190°C (fan oven 170°C), gas mark 5. Place the pheasant on a board, wrap the pancetta or bacon slices around the breasts and tie securely. This helps to keep the breast meat moist during roasting. Put the olives and fennel seeds into the pheasant cavity and secure with string.

2 Heat the butter and olive oil in a flameproof casserole over a medium heat and brown the pheasant slowly, turning frequently, for 20 minutes. Season with salt and pepper, and add the juniper berries. Pour in the wine and let it evaporate.

3 Add the chicken broth and place the casserole in the oven. Roast for about 30 minutes, basting frequently with the pan juices.

4 Cut the pheasant into serving pieces and arrange on a platter with the olives and fennel seeds. Place the casserole over a medium heat, add a little water or extra wine to deglaze and scrape up the browned bits from the bottom, using a wooden spoon. Pour this sauce through a sieve over the pheasant and serve, with a salad or vegetables of your choice.

pancetta

Of the many wonderful Italian cured meats, pancetta is arguably the most useful in cooking and increasingly popular. It is the cured *pancia*, meaning paunch or belly of the pig – the Italian equivalent of our streaky bacon, but much more flavoursome. You can also buy pancetta smoked, air-dried, and rolled with additional flavourings. It is sold by the piece, in slices, and ready diced in convenient packs with an extended shelf life.

Pancetta is usually fried and used as a base for sauces, including the famous carbonara (see right). Sliced pancetta is excellent for wrapping over the breasts of roasting birds, or around vegetables to be baked. The fat enriches, moisturises and adds a wonderful flavour. Fried cubes are the most important element of a *soffritto*, a combination of vegetable dice and pancetta, used as the starting point for many great Italian dishes. The following recipes illustrate the versatility of pancetta; each serves 4.

▲ **pancetta and vegetable spiedini**
Cut 250g (9oz) pancetta into fork-friendly pieces. Quarter 8 large field mushrooms. Cut a large, peeled red onion into wedges. Cut a large courgette into chunky rounds. Thread the pancetta, mushroom quarters, onion wedges and courgette chunks on to 4 skewers, interspersing with sage leaves. Cook under a preheated grill, basting frequently with olive oil, for 10–15 minutes until the vegetables and pancetta are cooked.

pancetta-wrapped stuffed chicken breasts

You need 4 chicken breast fillets with skin, each 150g (5oz), preferably corn-fed. Cut a deep pocket horizontally in each one. Fill each pocket with a few baby spinach leaves, 1 tbsp cream cheese and 2–3 sliced button mushrooms. Season well, then wrap each chicken breast in 2 slices of pancetta. Bake at 200°C, gas 6 for 20–25 minutes or until the pancetta is crisp and the chicken is cooked through. Serve with a green salad.

pancetta and tomato sauce (for pasta)

Fry a 130g double packet of pancetta cubes in 1 tbsp olive oil until crisp. Add 2 crushed garlic cloves, a handful of chopped sage leaves and 8 deseeded and chopped plum tomatoes. Cook gently for 6 minutes. Toss with 300–350g (11–12oz) freshly cooked dried pasta, such as bucatini or spaghetti. Serve scattered with 2 tbsp chopped flat leaf parsley and lots of freshly grated Parmesan.

▲ spaghetti carbonara

Fry 125g (4oz) pancetta dice with 1 finely chopped garlic clove in 1 tbsp olive oil until crisp; leave to cool. Cook 300–350g (11–12oz) dried spaghetti in the usual way. In a bowl, mix 2 very fresh large eggs with 142ml carton single cream and 2 tbsp freshly grated Parmesan, then add the pancetta with pan juices. Drain the cooked spaghetti, return to the pan and immediately pour in the carbonara sauce. Toss to coat and allow the egg to 'set' slightly. Serve with lots more Parmesan.

osso bucco con gremolata

This famous dish of stewed veal shanks originates from Lombardy. The pieces of veal are coated in seasoned flour, then braised in wine until meltingly tender. Here they are served topped with my tangy version of the typical gremolata accompaniment.
Illustrated on previous page

SERVES 6

6 pieces of veal shank (osso bucco), cut about
  4cm (1¹/₂ inches) thick
2–3 tablespoons plain flour, to dust
25g (1oz) unsalted butter
125ml (4 fl oz) dry white wine
finely pared zest and juice of 2 lemons
handful of flat leaf parsley, finely chopped
1 anchovy fillet in oil, drained and chopped
sea salt and freshly ground black pepper

1   Dredge the veal pieces in the flour, shaking off the excess. Melt the butter in a large, deep frying pan or sauté pan, then arrange the veal pieces in it. Brown over a medium heat, then turn carefully and brown the other side.

2   Pour in the wine and allow it to evaporate almost completely. Add some salt and pepper, cover tightly and cook very gently for about 1¹/₂ hours, adding a little water from time to time to keep some liquid in the bottom of the pan.

3   Chop the lemon zest and mix with the parsley; set aside. Add the anchovy and lemon juice to the stew. Sprinkle the lemon and parsley mix over the top and serve immediately.

beef braised in Barolo wine

Piedmont is renowned for its fine aged Barolo, and this is a traditional, robust dish from the region. It's an excellent way of braising beef for a special occasion. If possible, use Barolo that is at least five years old, which will give a wonderfully thick, tasty sauce. Otherwise, a good bottle of lesser full-bodied red wine will do.

SERVES 6

1kg (2¼lb) joint of braising beef (topside or
  top rump)
2 carrots, peeled and chopped
1 medium onion, peeled and roughly chopped
2 celery stalks, roughly chopped
handful of flat leaf parsley
3 bay leaves
1 tablespoon juniper berries
1 teaspoon black peppercorns
350ml (12fl oz) aged Barolo wine, or other
  full-bodied red wine
15g (½oz) unsalted butter, in pieces
1 tablespoon olive oil
sea salt and freshly ground black pepper

1 Put the meat into a bowl and add the chopped vegetables, herbs, juniper berries and peppercorns. Pour the wine over the meat, cover the bowl and marinate in the fridge for at least 24 hours.

2 Preheat the oven to 180°C (fan oven 160°C), gas mark 4. Remove the meat from the bowl and dry well, reserving the marinade. Make little slits in the surface of the meat and insert the pieces of butter. Strain the marinade, saving the vegetables and flavourings, as well as the liquor.

3 Heat the olive oil in a flameproof casserole. Add the meat and brown over a medium high heat on all sides.

4 Add the vegetables and flavourings to the meat. Add 250ml (8fl oz) of the reserved liquor and some salt. Cover and braise in the oven for about 3 hours, adding more of the reserved wine as needed to keep the meat from drying out.

5 When the meat is cooked, lift out and place on a warm platter; keep warm. Discard the bay leaves. Put the vegetables and other flavourings through a food mill with the cooking liquor (or whiz in a food processor). Reheat this sauce, check the seasoning and pour over the meat to serve.

steaks with pizzaiola sauce

Pizzaiola sauce is so called because it features the typical pizza ingredients – olive oil, garlic, oregano and tomatoes. It is always made with fresh tomatoes, cooked briefly until softened. This simple recipe is ideal for a special midweek supper, as it can be cooked very quickly when you return home from work.

SERVES 4

50ml (2 fl oz) olive oil
1 garlic clove, peeled
4 thin slices fillet steak, each about 150g (5oz)
400g (14oz) tomatoes, skinned, deseeded and
  coarsely chopped
1 tablespoon chopped oregano leaves, or
  2 teaspoons dried oregano
sea salt and freshly ground black pepper

TO SERVE:
few radicchio leaves, shredded (optional)
handful of rocket leaves

1   Heat the olive oil with the garlic in a heavy-based frying pan over a high heat. Add the meat and brown quickly on both sides.

2   Add the tomatoes, season with salt and pepper, and turn down the heat. Sprinkle the oregano over the meat and tomatoes, partially cover the pan and cook for 10 minutes.

3   Lift the tender pieces of meat from the pan and place on a warm plate; keep warm. Increase the heat and reduce the tomato sauce left in the pan by about half.

4   Serve the fillet steaks on a bed of shredded radicchio if you like, surrounded by the tomato sauce. Scatter a few rocket leaves on top and serve at once.

lamb braised with fennel and tomatoes

Wild fennel grows prolifically in Sardinia, and the rugged terrain is sheep country, so this combination of lamb and fennel seems natural and almost inevitable. The flavours complement each other well, the fennel helping to cut the richness of the lamb.

SERVES 6

1 boneless shoulder of lamb, about 1.4kg (3 lb)
50ml (2 fl oz) olive oil
1 onion, peeled and chopped
500g (1lb 2oz) canned peeled tomatoes
2 fennel bulbs, with fronds
sea salt and freshly ground black pepper

1 Trim the lamb of excess fat and cut into pieces, about 2cm (¾ inch) square. Heat the olive oil in a flameproof casserole, add the chopped onion and lamb pieces, and sauté over a medium high heat until the lamb cubes are browned all over.

2 Add the canned tomatoes to the casserole and season with salt and pepper. Cover and cook over a low heat for 10 minutes.

3 In the meantime, trim the fennel, reserving the feathery fronds, and cut into slices. Add the sliced fennel to the lamb and stir well. Cook, uncovered, for about an hour until the meat is tender, adding a little water to keep the meat moist if necessary from time to time.

4 Taste and adjust the seasoning. Finely chop some of the reserved fennel fronds and scatter over the braised lamb and fennel to serve.

pot roasted loin of pork

This is rather a grand dish, perfect for a dinner party. It's northern in influence, with Austrian touches like the juniper berries. The boned and rolled pork loin is pot-roasted in a sauce of wine, grappa and sage, until it is very tender, almost dropping off the bone.

SERVES 4–6

1 boned and rolled loin of pork, about
  1.5kg (3¼lb)
1 celery stalk
1 onion, peeled
1 small carrot, peeled
1 garlic clove, peeled
6 sage leaves

3 rosemary sprigs
2 tablespoons olive oil
150ml (¼ pint) dry white wine
3 tablespoons grappa (or vodka)
2 tablespoons juniper berries
250ml (8fl oz) vegetable broth (page 47)
sea salt and freshly ground pepper

1 Preheat the oven to 180°C (fan oven 160°C), gas mark 4. Season the pork loin with salt and pepper all over. Very finely chop the celery, onion, carrot, garlic, sage and leaves from 1 rosemary sprig.

2 Heat the olive oil in a flameproof casserole, add the pork and brown well on all sides. Lift the pork out and set aside on a large plate.

3 Add the chopped herbs, vegetables, garlic and a little salt to the casserole and sauté for 5 minutes. Place the meat on top. Increase the heat, pour over the wine and grappa and let bubble rapidly for a minute or so, turning the meat over once. Then add the juniper and half of the broth.

4 Cover the casserole and cook in the oven for 1½ hours or until tender, turning the meat twice and adding a little more broth if the vegetables appear too dry. To impart extra flavour, lay the other 2 rosemary sprigs on top of the pork about 15 minutes before the end of cooking.

5 To serve, remove the rind from the pork, then carve into slices. Strain the cooking juices and spoon them over and around the meat.

veal with pancetta and mushrooms

The rich, succulent flavour of this dish suggests that it has been cooking for hours, yet it is quick and easy to prepare for an after-work supper.

SERVES 4

130g packet diced pancetta

4 shallots, peeled and finely chopped

6 medium flat brown mushrooms, finely diced

knob of butter

6 tablespoons Marsala

handful of flat leaf parsley, finely chopped, plus
   extra to serve

4 veal escalopes, each about 115g (4oz)

sea salt and freshly ground black pepper

1 Put the pancetta dice into a large, wide sauté pan or frying pan and cook over a medium heat until the fat begins to run and the pancetta is golden at the edges. Add the shallots and cook for about 5 minutes until translucent. Add the mushrooms with the butter and cook until tender.

2 Increase the heat slightly and add half the Marsala, scraping up the sediment from the bottom of the pan with a wooden spoon. Add the parsley and seasoning. Remove with a slotted spoon; set aside.

3 Return the pan to the heat. When it is hot, add the veal escalopes with the remaining Marsala. Cook for 4 minutes on each side until tender and the liquid has evaporated. Serve topped with the pancetta and mushroom mixture, and scattered with a little chopped fresh parsley.

calf's liver Venetian style

Strips of calf's liver are fried very, very quickly in butter, and served with sweet onions braised in wine. This is a classic Venetian dish, known as *fegato alla veneziana*, and my mother's favourite.

SERVES 6

75g (3oz) unsalted butter

400g (14oz) onions, peeled and thinly sliced

125ml (4fl oz) dry white wine

800g (1¾lb) calf's liver, thinly sliced

sea salt and freshly ground black pepper

3 tablespoons chopped flat leaf parsley,
   to serve

1 Heat half the butter in a lidded frying pan, add the onions and cook for 5 minutes or until golden. Add the wine and some salt and pepper. Cover and braise the onions over a low heat until very tender, about 25 minutes, stirring every now and again. Remove the onions and keep warm.

2 In the meantime, remove any gristle or membrane from the calf's liver, then cut into strips.

3 When the onions are almost ready, melt the rest of the butter in another frying pan. Add the liver and sauté over a high heat just until cooked through, about 4 minutes. Add salt to taste, then mix with the braised onions. Serve immediately, scattered with parsley.

marinated venison stewed in red wine

In the northern Alto-Adige region, chamois, or small deer, are hunted, cooked and eaten during the shooting season. This special dish is typical of the region. The meat is marinated in full-bodied red wine with herbs before cooking, then served with a cream-enriched sauce made from the cooking liquor. Serve with 'wet' polenta (page 96) and grilled mushrooms.

SERVES 6

1.4kg (3lb) boneless stewing venison
4 tablespoons olive oil
2 tablespoons plain flour
50g (2oz) pancetta (preferably smoked), diced
1 onion, peeled and chopped
1/2 teaspoon ground cinnamon
1/2 teaspoon ground cloves
284ml carton soured cream
sea salt and freshly ground black pepper

FOR THE MARINADE:

1 carrot, peeled and cut into pieces
1 large onion, peeled and coarsely sliced
1 celery stalk, cut into pieces
1 tablespoon coarse sea salt
2 tablespoons juniper berries, crushed
8 black peppercorns, bruised
3 cloves
1 rosemary sprig
3 tablespoons olive oil
3 bay leaves
3 garlic cloves, peeled
1 bottle Barolo or other full-bodied red wine

1 Put all the ingredients for the marinade into a large bowl. Cut the venison into 5cm (2 inches) pieces and add to the marinade. Stir well, then cover and leave to marinate in the refrigerator for about 12 hours.

2 Using a slotted spoon, lift the meat from the marinade, drain and pat dry with kitchen paper. Strain the marinade and reserve. Preheat the oven to 190°C (fan oven 170°C), gas mark 5.

3 Heat 2 tablespoons olive oil in a large heavy-based frying pan. Working in batches, brown the meat all over, then transfer to a side plate. Add the flour to the pan and cook until brown, stirring and scraping up the sediment on the bottom of the pan. Gradually stir in about half of the strained marinade and bring to the boil, stirring constantly.

4 Heat the remaining 2 tablespoons olive oil in a large flameproof casserole and fry the pancetta for 5 minutes. Add the onion with a pinch of salt and cook until it is soft.

5 Now add the meat with its juices, the wine sauce from the frying pan and about 150ml (1/4 pint) of the remaining marinade. Season with salt and pepper, and add the ground spices. Bring slowly to the boil, then cover the casserole and place in the oven. Cook for about an hour or until the meat is almost tender, adding a little more of the marinade twice during the cooking.

6 Add the soured cream to the casserole. Return to the oven and cook for a further 30 minutes or longer, until the meat is very tender. The cooking time will depend on the age of the animal.

7 vegetables and salads

baked onions with prosciutto and Parmesan

A delicious, rib-sticking winter dish from Lombardy, which can be prepared in advance ready to pop into the oven. The onions are stuffed with breadcrumbs flavoured with plenty of prosciutto and Parmesan, then baked until sweet and tender. Serve as an antipasto in the winter, or as a vegetable side dish.

SERVES 4 or 8

8 large white onions, peeled
2 tablespoons coarse white breadcrumbs
1/2 tablespoon milk
150g (5oz) prosciutto, finely chopped
6 tablespoons freshly grated Parmesan cheese
1 medium egg, beaten
15g (1/2oz) unsalted butter, in pieces, plus extra
   to grease
sea salt and freshly ground black pepper

1 Add the onions to a pan of boiling salted water and simmer for 15 minutes. Meanwhile, soak the breadcrumbs in the milk. Preheat the oven to 180°C (fan oven 160°C), gas mark 4.

2 Drain the onions, reserving the liquid. Rinse under cold running water, then drain and pat dry with kitchen paper. Cut a thin slice from the top of each onion and scoop out the centres, using a teaspoon; keep half of the onion flesh that you remove. Place the onion 'cups' upside down on a board while you prepare the filling.

3 Finely chop the reserved onion. Squeeze the breadcrumbs to remove excess liquid and place in a bowl with the onion. Add the prosciutto, Parmesan and beaten egg. Season with salt and pepper and mix well. Spoon the stuffing into the onion shells.

4 Grease a baking dish with butter and arrange the onions in it. Dot with butter and moisten the onions with 50ml (2fl oz) of the reserved cooking liquid. Bake for 40 minutes, basting the onions from time to time with the pan juices. Serve hot.

cabbage leaves stuffed with leeks and mushrooms

Stuffed vegetables are commonplace in Italy, and most recipes come from around Rome. Here, though, the aspect is more northern, in that cabbage is used. These attractive little bundles can be assembled ahead of time, and the filling can be as varied as you like – try mozzarella and anchovies, for instance.

SERVES 4

1 Savoy cabbage
225g (8oz) leeks, washed and trimmed
125g (4oz) flat field mushrooms, wiped
25g (1oz) unsalted butter
2 garlic cloves, peeled and finely chopped

50g (2oz) slivered almonds
2–3 teaspoons lemon juice
2 teaspoons paprika
1 medium egg, beaten
150ml (¼ pint) vegetable broth (page 47)
sea salt and freshly ground black pepper

1 Preheat the oven to 200°C (fan oven 180°C), gas mark 6. Select 8 large, darker outer leaves from the cabbage. Blanch these leaves in boiling salted water, or steam, for 1–2 minutes to soften slightly. Cut away the tough centre stalks.

2 Finely chop the leeks, mushrooms and 225g (8oz) of the remaining cabbage. Melt the butter in a large frying pan. Add the garlic, leeks, mushrooms and chopped cabbage and fry gently, stirring frequently, for 10 minutes.

3 Add the almonds, lemon juice and paprika to the leek mixture and cook over a low heat for 5 minutes. Remove from the heat and allow to cool. Add the beaten egg and some salt and pepper to the cooled stuffing and mix well.

4 Divide the stuffing between the blanched cabbage leaves and roll up tightly, tucking in the sides as you roll. Pack the cabbage parcels into an ovenproof dish, placing them join-side down. Pour the vegetable broth around them and cover the dish with foil. Bake in the oven for 20 minutes. Serve hot.

Roman artichokes

Artichokes grow all over Italy, but the Lazio region, and Rome in particular, is especially renowned for its small, tender artichokes. Speciality dishes feature on restaurant menus throughout the capital during the artichoke season. Try to buy young artichokes with long stalks, as these are tender and won't yet have developed much in the way of a choke. For this starter the artichokes are best served warm.

Illustrated on previous page

SERVES 4

4 medium artichokes
l lemon, cut in half
3 bay leaves
150ml (¼ pint) dry white wine
FOR THE DRESSING:
large handful of mint leaves
2 garlic cloves, peeled
3–4 tablespoons extra virgin olive oil
2 tablespoons white wine vinegar
sea salt and freshly ground black pepper

1 Prepare the artichokes one at a time. Trim the base of the stalk at an angle, then peel the stem. Cut off the leaves about 5mm (¼ inch) from the top. Rub the cut surfaces with a lemon half. Now start peeling away the artichoke leaves, removing at least four layers, until the leaves begin to look pale. Spread the top leaves and reach down with a teaspoon to scrape out the choke. Immerse the artichoke in a bowl of cold water with the other lemon half added (to prevent discoloration). Repeat to prepare the rest of the artichokes.

2 Place the bay leaves, lemon halves, wine and artichokes in a large pan and add enough cold water to cover. (The artichokes should fit snugly in the pan.) Bring to the boil, cover and simmer for about 30–35 minutes until the artichokes are tender. Drain thoroughly.

3 To make the dressing, chop the mint leaves very finely together with the garlic, then place in a bowl with the olive oil, wine vinegar and salt and pepper to taste. Whisk to blend thoroughly.

4 Arrange the artichokes upside down (with their stalks sticking up) on serving plates. While still warm, pour over the dressing and serve.

creamy potato casserole with prosciutto

This is very similar to the French *gratin dauphinoise*, and it's ideal served after (or with) a simple meat dish. A little finely chopped garlic can be added to increase the flavour, or for a more subtle taste, rub a cut garlic clove around the dish with the butter. The casserole may be prepared and baked ahead, and reheated to serve.

SERVES 6

1kg (2¹/₄lb) old potatoes (such as Maris Piper,
   King Edward, Pentland Crown)
25g (1oz) unsalted butter
125g (4oz) prosciutto slices
450ml (³/₄ pint) milk
250ml (8fl oz) single cream
225g (8oz) Parmesan cheese, freshly grated
freshly grated nutmeg, to taste
sea salt and freshly ground black pepper

1 Preheat the oven to 180°C (fan oven 160°C), gas mark 4. Peel the potatoes and slice them thinly. Grease a large shallow baking dish with half of the butter. Lay the potato slices in the dish, overlapping them slightly. Lay the slices of prosciutto on top.

2 In a bowl, mix together the milk, cream and half of the grated Parmesan, and season with nutmeg, salt and pepper. Pour the mixture over the potatoes. Sprinkle with the remaining Parmesan and dot with the rest of the butter.

3 Bake in the oven until the potatoes are tender, about 45 minutes. If necessary, increase the oven temperature towards the end of the baking time to brown the crust. Serve hot.

Neapolitan vegetable casserole

Known locally as *ciambotta*, this is Naples' answer to ratatouille. It's an easy dish, and one that can be cooked ahead of time. Vary the vegetables as you like – perhaps adding celery or fennel.

SERVES 4

1 medium aubergine
1 medium onion, peeled
1 red pepper
2 medium potatoes, peeled
1 courgette, trimmed
3 tablespoons olive oil
1 garlic clove, peeled and crushed
2–3 teaspoons fennel seeds, crushed
400g can peeled plum tomatoes
6 tablespoons red wine
2 teaspoons dried oregano
sea salt and freshly ground black pepper

1 Cut the aubergine into cubes. Sprinkle with salt, place in a colander, cover and weight down. Leave to degorge the bitter juices for 15 minutes.

2 Meanwhile, chop the onion. Halve, core and deseed the red pepper. Cut the red pepper, potatoes and courgette into similar sized chunks. Rinse the aubergine cubes and pat dry.

3 Heat the olive oil in a saucepan, add the onion and cook gently for about 5 minutes or until softened, then add the garlic and cook for a minute. Add all the vegetables and remaining ingredients. Bring to a simmer and cook gently for 25–30 minutes until the vegetables are tender, adding a little water to moisten during cooking if necessary. Serve hot.

peas with spring onions and pancetta

Freshly podded young peas are cooked together quickly with sautéed spring onions and chopped salty Italian bacon in one pan. This is how Italians appreciate the sweet flavour of our most popular vegetable.

Illustrated right

SERVES 4–6

2 tablespoons olive oil

2 bunches of spring onions, trimmed and
  roughly chopped

150g (5oz) pancetta, diced

500g (1lb 2oz) podded fresh or frozen peas
  (preferably fresh)

handful of flat leaf parsley, chopped, plus a
  sprig to serve

sea salt and freshly ground black pepper

1   Heat the olive oil in a large frying pan over a medium heat. Add the spring onions and pancetta and sauté until the onions are translucent.

2   Add the peas, salt, pepper and 125ml (4fl oz) boiling water. Bring to a simmer and cook uncovered until the peas are tender, about 5–7 minutes for fresh peas, 3–4 minutes for frozen ones.

3   Drain the peas and toss with the chopped parsley. Transfer to a warm bowl and top with the parsley sprig to serve.

braised fennel with pecorino

Fennel is sautéed in butter and olive oil until tender, then served topped with pecorino cheese shavings. This tempting dish is especially good after fish.

SERVES 4

2 fennel bulbs, with fronds

25g (1oz) unsalted butter

1 tablespoon olive oil

150g (5oz) pecorino cheese, pared into shavings

sea salt and freshly ground black pepper

1   Trim the fennel bulbs, reserving a few of the feathery fronds for garnish. Cut each fennel bulb in half from top to bottom and blanch in boiling salted water for 5 minutes, then drain.

2   Melt the butter with the olive oil in a heavy-based sauté pan or frying pan over a medium heat. Add the halved fennel bulbs and cook for 10–12 minutes or until tender and golden brown, turning from time to time to colour evenly. Season with salt and pepper.

3   Transfer to a warm serving plate and scatter with pecorino shavings. Garnish with the fennel fronds and serve at once.

salad leaves and dressings

Italians love their salads. They are regarded as a digestive, a healthy way to settle the stomach, so a side salad often follows the main course. Typically this is a selection of salad leaves with a simple dressing of good extra virgin olive oil and lemon juice or vinegar, and seasoning.

Many fine salad leaves originate from Italy, including peppery rocket, lollo rosso, lollo biondo and radicchio. Often the shape and texture of the leaves dictates the style of dressing: sturdier leaves can take a thicker dressing. Only use very fresh salad leaves. Wash them just before preparing the salad, then drain and carefully pat dry with kitchen paper.

Of course, other ingredients can be added to salads for texture and flavour, including cooked vegetables such as aubergines, artichoke hearts and fennel, tomatoes and other fruits, freshly chopped herbs, olives, anchovies, capers, pine nuts, sun-dried tomatoes and small pieces of bread.

▲ **all-purpose Italian dressing**
This is my all-time favourite dressing, which I use to dress bitter leaves, such as frisée and rocket, as well as crisp Cos or Little Gem lettuce. In a bowl, mix the juice and finely grated zest of 1 lemon, a crushed ½ garlic clove, 4 tbsp extra virgin olive oil, salt and pepper. Whisk to combine. Add about 1 tbsp freshly grated Parmesan cheese, which immediately makes the dressing thicker and creamier. Use at once, whiz in a blender or food processor for a smoother dressing.

basic balsamic vinaigrette

You can use this vinaigrette to dress meats and vegetables, as well as salad leaves. In a bowl, mix 30ml (2 tbsp) good, aged balsamic vinegar with 125ml (4 fl oz) extra virgin olive oil, or a combination of olive and sunflower or other oil of your choice. Season with salt and pepper and whisk well. Balsamic jelly (sold in a jar) can be used instead of the vinegar; dilute it to taste with oil, to make your dressing as thick as you like.

anchovy-based dressing

Use this to dress rocket, spinach, lollo rosso, radicchio and any member of the endive family. Gently heat 125ml (4 fl oz) fruity extra virgin olive oil in a small pan, then add a finely chopped shallot and sweat until soft. Add 6 chopped anchovies, 175ml (6 fl oz) dry white wine, a finely chopped garlic clove, and a handful of torn basil leaves. Gently warm through, then whiz in a blender or food processor until smooth. Pass through a fine sieve and season to taste (but go easy with the salt).

▲ Sicilian salad

A refreshing salad dressed with fruity olive oil. To prepare, peel and slice 6 oranges (blood oranges when in season) into thin rounds. Trim and slice a medium fennel bulb; save a few feathery fronds. Combine the fennel and oranges, snipped fennel fronds and 3 tbsp chopped fresh walnuts. Dress with 2 tbsp extra virgin olive oil, season with salt and pepper, and leave to stand for an hour or so, turning occasionally. Serve with a few Cos lettuce leaves.

marinated courgettes

This is a typical southern recipe from Campania. Finely sliced courgettes are oven-dried, then fried and marinated in wine vinegar and fruity olive oil with freshly chopped mint. For optimum flavour, marinate the courgettes overnight.

SERVES 6
9 large courgettes, trimmed
175ml (6 fl oz) olive oil
FOR THE DRESSING:
large handful of mint leaves, coarsely chopped
3 garlic cloves, peeled and finely chopped
6 tablespoons white wine vinegar
4 tablespoons extra virgin olive oil
sea salt

1 Preheat the oven to 140°C (fan oven 120°C), gas mark 1, and line two large baking trays with baking parchment.

2 Cut the courgettes lengthways into thin slices and place in a single layer on the lined trays. Leave in the oven for about an hour to dry out completely without colouring.

3 Heat the olive oil in a large frying pan and fry the courgettes in batches until golden; there's no need to turn them. Drain carefully on kitchen paper.

4 Transfer the courgette slices to a serving bowl and sprinkle with the chopped mint and garlic. Drizzle over the wine vinegar and extra virgin olive oil, and season with salt to taste. Cover and leave to stand for 2 hours before serving or, better still, overnight.

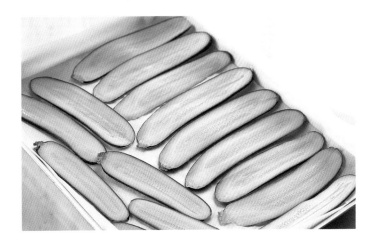

caponata

The secret of this classic *agro dolce* (sweet sour) Sicilian dish is to cook the aubergines separately and combine them with the tomato sauce at the last moment, so their individual flavour is retained. Flavoured with olives, capers and pine nuts, the caponata can be served hot or cold, as an antipasto or vegetable dish. It will keep well in the refrigerator for several days.

SERVES 4

2 medium aubergines
4 tablespoons olive oil
1 onion, peeled and sliced
400g can chopped tomatoes, drained
3 celery stalks, trimmed
1 tablespoon capers, rinsed
50g (2oz) pitted green olives, rinsed
4 tablespoons white wine vinegar
1 tablespoon caster sugar
2 tablespoons pine nuts
handful of flat leaf parsley, chopped
sea salt and freshly ground black pepper

1 Cut the aubergines into 2.5cm (1 inch) cubes. Sprinkle with salt, place in a colander, cover and weight down. Leave to degorge the bitter juices for 15 minutes, then rinse to remove the salt and pat dry with kitchen paper.

2 Heat 3 tablespoons of the olive oil in a large frying pan. Add the aubergine cubes and fry, turning, until brown and tender. Drain on kitchen paper, and keep to one side.

3 Heat the remaining 1 tablespoon olive oil in a saucepan, add the onion and fry for 5 minutes until golden. Add the tomatoes and some salt and pepper, and simmer for 15 minutes.

4 Meanwhile, cut the celery into 1cm (½ inch) pieces. Add to the tomato sauce with the capers, olives, vinegar and sugar. Simmer for a further 15 minutes until reduced slightly, stirring occasionally.

5 Put the aubergine and pine nuts into a serving dish and pour over the tomato sauce. Stir, then leave to stand for at least 30 minutes. Scatter with the chopped parsley just before serving.

Tuscan cabbage and cannellini beans on toast

This dish can be served as a starter or antipasto, or as a vegetable. The contrast of the black cabbage and white cannellini beans makes it visually appealing. Dress the whole lot with new season's extra virgin olive oil to bring out all the flavours. If you haven't time to cook dried beans, use a 400g can cannellini beans instead; drain, rinse and flavour with a little crushed garlic and chopped thyme.

SERVES 6

200g (7oz) dried white cannellini beans,
  soaked in cold water overnight
2 rosemary sprigs
3 bay leaves
3 thyme sprigs
3 flat leaf parsley sprigs
4 garlic cloves, unpeeled
450g (1lb) cavolo nero (or green cabbage),
  stalks removed
6 slightly dry slices of fine-textured, country
  style bread
extra virgin olive oil, to drizzle
sea salt and freshly ground black pepper

1 Drain the cannellini beans and place in a large pan. Add plenty of cold water to cover, the herbs and 3 unpeeled garlic cloves. Bring to the boil, then reduce the heat and cook for about 1½ hours or until the beans are tender.

2 Preheat the oven to 200°C (fan oven 180°C), gas mark 6. Roughly chop the cavolo nero leaves and add to a pan of boiling salted water. Return to the boil and simmer for 10–15 minutes until tender.

3 Arrange the bread slices in a single layer on a baking sheet and bake in the oven for 3 minutes. Turn them over and bake for a further 3 minutes. In the meantime, peel and halve the remaining garlic clove. While the bread is hot, rub one side with the garlic.

4 Drain the beans and discard the herbs and garlic. Arrange the bread on a plate, garlic side up. Scoop the cavolo nero from the pan using a slotted spoon, drain well and arrange on the bread slices. Spoon the hot cannellini beans on top. Drizzle with extra virgin olive oil, season with salt and pepper and serve immediately.

8 desserts and sweets

meringues with chocolate sauce

Classic Italian meringue has a wonderful silky texture, but it does involve boiling sugar syrup and the use of a sugar thermometer, so I have opted for the easier alternative here. This simple method produces meringues that are crisp on the outside. Sandwich them together with cream and serve with a luxurious chocolate sauce.

SERVES 4

3 egg whites
175g (6oz) caster sugar
250ml (8fl oz) double cream

FOR THE CHOCOLATE SAUCE:
200g (7oz) luxury dark chocolate, broken
  into pieces
125ml (4fl oz) milk

1 Preheat the oven to its lowest setting, 110°C (fan oven 100°C), gas mark ¼. Line a large baking sheet with baking parchment.

2 Whisk the egg whites in a clean bowl until stiff and glossy. With patience, add the sugar very gradually, whisking well between each addition. The meringue should be stiff and shiny.

3 Spoon the meringue into a piping bag fitted with a 2.5cm (1 inch) plain tip and pipe about 16 mounds, about 5cm (2 inches) in diameter, on the baking sheet, spacing them well apart.

4 Bake the meringues in the oven for about 2 hours until crisp and dry, but still white. Peel the meringues away from the paper and place on a wire rack. Leave to cool completely.

5 For the sauce, melt the chocolate with the milk in a heatproof bowl set over a pan of gently simmering water. Take off the heat and stir until smooth. Cool slightly, or completely if you prefer to serve the sauce at room temperature.

6 To assemble, whip the cream until it holds soft peaks. Sandwich the cold meringues together in pairs with the cream, then arrange on a serving dish. Pour the warm or cool chocolate sauce over the meringues and serve.

grilled fruit salad with zabaglione sauce

Fresh seasonal fruits – especially peaches, nectarines, cherries and pears – are often served at the end of a meal in Italy. As an alternative, I sometimes serve a medley of fruits under a caramelised zabaglione topping. The result is delicious, and not dissimilar to a fruit crème brûlée. Either use a large shallow baking dish or individual gratin dishes.

SERVES 4
100g (3½oz) strawberries, hulled
1 kiwi fruit
1 pear
100g (3½oz) raspberries
2 tablespoons Vin Santo (or
   1 tablespoon Marsala)

FOR THE ZABAGLIONE:
3 egg yolks
75g (3oz) caster sugar
2½ tablespoons Marsala

TO FINISH:
1–2 teaspoons icing sugar, sifted, to sprinkle

1 Halve or slice the strawberries. Peel and slice the kiwi fruit. Peel, core and slice the pear. Leave the raspberries whole. Combine the fruit in an ovenproof baking dish (or individual grillproof dishes) and sprinkle with the Vin Santo or Marsala.

2 To make the zabaglione, put the egg yolks and caster sugar into a heatproof bowl and whisk until creamy and almost white in colour. Gradually add the Marsala, whisking constantly until the mixture is well combined.

3 Place the bowl over a saucepan of simmering water and cook over a medium heat, beating constantly with the whisk, until the zabaglione is creamy and thick.

4 Pour the hot zabaglione over the fruit. Sprinkle with icing sugar. Place under a preheated hot grill for 30 seconds, or wave a blow-torch over the surface until the zabaglione begins to brown. Serve immediately, with vanilla ice cream if you wish.

baked stuffed peaches

The Mediterranean climate is ideal for growing peaches and Italian peaches, in particular, are prized for their juicy, fragrant flesh. This recipe is a classic from Lombardy. Halved peaches are stuffed with a mixture of ground almonds, crumbled amaretti and cocoa powder, then drizzled with dry white wine and baked until tender.

Illustrated on previous page

SERVES 4

4 large ripe peaches
9 amaretti biscuits, crushed
25g (1oz) ground almonds
1 egg yolk
1 tablespoon cocoa powder, sifted
300ml (1/2 pint) dry white wine
2 tablespoons soft brown sugar

1 Preheat the oven to 180°C (fan oven 160°C), gas mark 4. Wash the peaches and pat dry. Cut them in half following the natural line and remove the stone. Using a teaspoon, scoop out a little of the pulp from the middle of each peach half to create a cavity. Finely chop the scooped-out pulp.

2 In a bowl, combine the chopped peach pulp, crushed amaretti biscuits, ground almonds, egg yolk and cocoa powder, and mix thoroughly until evenly blended. (Alternatively, whiz in a food processor for a few seconds until smooth.)

3 Fill the peach cavities with the almond mixture and place side by side in a baking dish. Pour the wine over the peaches, sprinkle with the brown sugar and bake in the oven for 25 minutes.

4 Allow the peaches to cool and serve at room temperature, drizzled with the cooking juices.

coffee zabaglione

Zabaglione is the most famous classic Italian dessert, made from egg yolks, sugar and Marsala – the vital flavouring ingredient. Over the years, new ways of serving zabaglione have evolved (see page 172), and you come across different flavour variations in Italy. Here I have added espresso coffee for a delicious twist. Serve the zabaglione warm, with seasonal fruit if you like, or freeze it to make a wonderful ice cream that freezes to a soft texture, rather than ice hard. Note that this recipe uses lightly cooked egg yolks (see note on page 5).

SERVES 4

4 large egg yolks
2 tablespoons golden caster sugar
pinch of Italian '00' flour or plain flour
2 tablespoons freshly made espresso coffee
1 teaspoon whole milk
50ml (2 fl oz) dry Marsala

1   Combine the egg yolks, sugar and flour in a large heatproof bowl and place over a pan of gently simmering water, making sure the base of the bowl is not in direct contact with the water. Beat constantly, using a balloon whisk. As the sugar dissolves, the mixture will become runny, then as it cooks the zabaglione thickens to the consistency of double cream. This takes about 5 minutes.

2   At this point, pour in the espresso, milk and Marsala. Continue to beat with the balloon whisk until the zabaglione becomes thick and fluffy. This should take about 5 minutes.

3   Remove the bowl from the pan and allow the zabaglione to rest for 10 minutes. Spoon into glasses and serve warm.

4   Alternatively, cool and freeze in a shallow container, covered, for 3 hours. Whisk and re-freeze for 2 hours or until firm. Serve scooped into glasses.

ricotta cheesecake with strawberry sauce

This baked cheesecake has a superb texture and flavour, which is partly due to the ricotta – Italy's light, versatile soft cheese. The accompanying strawberry purée adds a sweet, refreshing note. You could also fold some chopped nuts or raisins into the ricotta filling if you like.

SERVES 6

FOR THE PASTRY:
275g (10oz) Italian '00' flour, plus extra to dust
50g (2oz) caster sugar
125g (4oz) unsalted butter, softened
1 egg, plus 1 egg yolk
1/2 teaspoon vanilla extract
finely grated zest of 1 small unwaxed lemon
1/2 teaspoon baking powder

FOR THE FILLING:
2 eggs, separated
125g (4oz) granulated sugar
50g (2oz) unsalted butter, softened
finely grated zest of 1 unwaxed lemon
1 teaspoon vanilla extract
275g (10oz) ricotta cheese
1 teaspoon thin honey
1 teaspoon baking powder

FOR THE SAUCE:
150g (5oz) strawberries, hulled
juice of 1 lemon
1 tablespoon caster sugar

1 To make the pastry, combine all the ingredients in a food processor and process until the mixture is evenly blended and comes together as a ball of dough. If the pastry is a little too sticky, add a bit more flour. Wrap the dough in cling film and leave to rest in the refrigerator for about 30 minutes.

2 Preheat the oven to 150°C (fan oven 130°C), gas mark 2. Roll out the pastry on a lightly floured surface to a 3mm (1/8 inch) thickness and use to line a 20cm (8 inch) springform tin, or deep loose-based flan tin, pressing the pastry on to the bottom and up the sides. Set aside.

3 For the filling, beat the egg yolks, sugar, butter, lemon zest and vanilla together with an electric mixer until smooth. Add the ricotta, honey and baking powder and mix gently until evenly blended. In a separate bowl, whisk the egg whites until they hold firm peaks, then gently fold into the filling.

4 Pour the filling into the pastry case and bake in the oven for 2 1/2 hours. Leave to cool in the tin on a wire rack. Chill until ready to serve.

5 For the sauce, purée the strawberries, lemon juice and sugar in a blender, then pass through a sieve into a bowl. Cover and chill for 30 minutes.

6 Carefully unmould the cheesecake on to a flat plate. Serve in slices, topped with a ladleful of strawberry sauce.

almond pudding with bitter chocolate sauce

This is a very old recipe, dating back to the Middle Ages. Almonds were introduced by the Arabs into Sicily during their occupation of southern Italy and they feature in this pudding. A dark chocolate sauce complements the flavour well.

SERVES 4

200g (7oz) blanched almonds
grated zest of 1 unwaxed lemon
2 teaspoons powdered gelatine
375ml (13fl oz) milk
125g (4oz) caster sugar
1 teaspoon vanilla extract
1 tablespoon Grand Marnier
125g (4oz) dark, bitter chocolate, finely chopped

1 Put the blanched almonds into a blender or food processor and grind to a fine paste. Transfer to a bowl and stir in 175ml (6fl oz) warm water and the lemon zest. Mix thoroughly and set aside to rest for 1 hour. Strain the almond liquid through a sieve into a bowl.

2 Sprinkle the gelatine over 1 tablespoon cold water in a bowl and leave to soften for 5 minutes. Pour 150ml (¼ pint) of the milk into a saucepan and add the sugar and vanilla extract. Slowly bring to the boil over a low heat, stirring to dissolve the sugar. Add the gelatine and whisk briefly to dissolve.

3 Take off the heat and add the almond liquid, Grand Marnier and remaining milk. Mix well, then pour into a 25cm (10 inch) ring mould or 1 litre (1¾ pint) pudding basin and refrigerate for 3 hours.

4 Melt the chocolate in a bowl set over a pan of hot water. Stir until melted and very smooth. Remove the bowl from the pan and allow to cool slightly.

5 Briefly dip the mould into hot water, then turn out the pudding on to a serving plate. Drizzle some of the melted chocolate sauce on top; hand the rest separately.

my grandmother's espresso pudding

This very simple dessert, which is rather like a coffee crème caramel, has been in my family for generations, and my grandmother often made it. She was very frugal, and would always use leftover coffee in ice creams, baked puddings and cakes.

SERVES 4

450ml (3/4 pint) brewed espresso coffee, cooled
150g (5oz) caster sugar
5 large eggs, beaten
1 teaspoon lemon juice
350ml (12 fl oz) double cream

1 Combine the cooled espresso and half the sugar in a large bowl and stir well. Add the beaten eggs, a little at a time, mixing thoroughly.

2 Put the remaining sugar, the lemon juice and 1 tablespoon water into a small heavy-based pan. Cook over a medium to high heat until the mixture turns a pale caramel colour. Immediately pour the caramel into a shallow 25cm (10 inch) ring mould or 1 litre (1¾ pint) shallow round baking dish, tilting it in all directions to distribute the caramel over the bottom and sides. Continue to tilt until the caramel has hardened. Leave to cool for 30 minutes.

3 Preheat the oven to 180°C (fan oven 160°C), gas mark 4. Pour the coffee mixture into the caramel-lined mould and place in a large roasting tin containing enough water to come halfway up the sides of the mould. Bake in the oven for 1 hour until the pudding is set and a toothpick or wooden cocktail stick inserted in the centre comes out dry. Allow the pudding to cool for 1 hour.

4 To serve, unmould on to a serving plate. Whip the cream until thick and pile into the centre (if you have used a ring mould), or serve individual portions with a dollop of whipped cream.

apple cake

This light Genoese sponge layered with apples is delicious with coffee for breakfast, or for an afternoon snack. To vary the flavour, try adding a little finely chopped fresh rosemary to the mix.

SERVES 6–8

1–2 teaspoons vegetable oil
1–2 tablespoons dried breadcrumbs
125g (4oz) unsalted butter
500g (1lb 2oz) Golden Delicious apples
4 eggs
150g (5oz) caster sugar

150g (5oz) Italian '00' flour
1 teaspoon baking powder
pinch of salt
6 tablespoons milk
finely grated zest of 2 unwaxed lemons
icing sugar, sifted, to dust
rosemary sprigs, to finish (optional)

1 Preheat the oven to 180°C (fan oven 160°C), gas mark 4. Brush the inside of a 23cm (9 inch) cake tin with the oil, then sprinkle with the breadcrumbs and shake off the excess. Melt the butter and set aside to cool. Peel, quarter and core the apples, then slice thinly.

2 Put the eggs and sugar into a heatproof bowl over a pan of gently simmering water. Whisk for 10–15 minutes until the mixture is thick and pale, and leaves a trail when the beaters are lifted. Remove the bowl from the heat and continue whisking until the mixture is cool.

3 Sift the flour with the baking powder and salt. Fold half of this mixture gently into the whisked eggs and sugar. Slowly trickle the melted butter around the edge of the bowl and fold it in gently. Take care to avoid knocking out the air and losing volume. Fold in the remaining flour mixture, then the milk and lemon zest, and finally the apple slices.

4 Pour the mixture into the prepared tin. Bake for 45 minutes or until a skewer inserted in the centre comes out clean. Leave in the tin for 5 minutes, then turn out on to a wire rack and leave to cool. To serve, dust the top of the cake liberally with icing sugar and scatter with rosemary sprigs if liked.

cheeses

Italy produces many superb cheeses. Aged, hard Parmesan and creamy blue Gorgonzola are famous the world over; other excellent varieties include pecorino (from sheep's milk), mozzarella (from buffalo milk) and soft, creamy ricotta.

Cheese is used a great deal in cooking, but it is also eaten as a course on its own, often instead of a dessert. Typically a generous wedge of one excellent cheese is served with fruit such as grapes, apples or pears, or nuts, or a crisp salad vegetable. Of course, you can serve a selection of cheeses if you prefer.

In the south we finish a meal with a local cheese plus some celery or fennel, or fresh nuts. An unusual Italian custom is to serve a sharp cheese topped with fruit or nuts and drizzled with a little honey. This is eaten with a knife and fork. Pecorino, honey and walnuts is a classic combination; the contrast of saltiness and sweetness is wonderful.

▲ pecorino and fennel salad

To serve 4, thinly slice 2 small fennel bulbs and shave 400g (14 oz) pecorino romano cheese into wafer-thin slices, using a swivel vegetable peeler. Arrange the cheese, fennel and a handful of rocket leaves on 4 plates. Scatter a small handful of toasted pine nuts on top. Drizzle with 3 tbsp extra virgin olive oil and sprinkle with black pepper and a little sea salt.

Sardinian cheese biscuits

Make these to serve with cheese. Mound 150g (5oz) semolina or Italian '00' flour on a work surface and make a well in the middle. Add a small egg, 75g (3oz) grated pecorino cheese and a pinch of salt. Mix together, adding enough water (about 4 tbsp) to make a soft dough. Break into small pieces, roll into balls, then flatten to very thin discs. Deep-fry in hot olive oil for about 5–6 minutes until golden. Drain well.

Italian cheese and balsamic jelly

Balsamic jelly is one of my recent discoveries. Sold in jars, it is available from selected supermarkets. It tastes wonderful and is the ideal complement to full flavoured Italian cheeses, such as Gorgonzola or a sharp pecorino. Serve a wedge of either cheese with a generous spoonful of balsamic jelly, and grapes or pear if you like.

▲ Gorgonzola, pear and toasted walnuts

To serve 4, roast 12 fresh walnuts in the oven at 200°C, gas 6 for 5–7 minutes; don't let them burn. Peel and core 4 pears, and then cut into thin wedges. Arrange the pear wedges on 4 plates, and crumble over 125g (4oz) Gorgonzola cheese. Top with the toasted walnuts and drizzle over some fragrant thin honey.

chocolate coated figs with almond stuffing

Figs are plentiful in Italy and this dried fruit delicacy, *fichi mandorlati*, comes from the Calabria region. The attractive chocolate-dipped figs make an ideal foodie gift, especially at Christmas. For best results, use good quality dried figs, and massage them lightly with your fingers to plump them up before stuffing.

MAKES 12

12 whole blanched almonds
finely pared zest of 3 oranges
12 dried figs, preferably Italian
225g (8oz) luxury dark chocolate

1   Preheat the grill to medium. Spread the almonds on a foil-lined grill pan and toast under the grill until golden, turning frequently and watching carefully to make sure they don't burn. Allow to cool.

2   Chop the orange zest very finely and scatter on a board. Slit the figs vertically and place an almond inside each one. Roll the figs in the orange zest to coat all over.

3   Meanwhile, break the chocolate into pieces and put in a heatproof bowl over a saucepan of simmering water. Leave until melted, then take off the heat and stir until smooth.

4   One at a time, spear the figs with a fork and partially dip in the chocolate, turning to coat all round. Place on a sheet of baking parchment and leave to dry.

chocolate salami

This sweetmeat comes from Emilia-Romagna, where the cooks are incredibly creative. It's a combination of chocolate, nuts, biscuits and brandy, which is rolled into a sausage, chilled until set and then sliced. You can make the rolls as fat or thin as you like, but never huge as the mixture is very rich! Smaller discs make ideal petits fours. Serve with coffee.

SERVES 4–6

90g (3¼oz) raisins
225g (8oz) luxury dark chocolate
50g (2oz) unsalted butter
50g (2oz) caster sugar
90g (3¼oz) blanched whole almonds,
  coarsely chopped
225g (8oz) Petit Beurre type biscuits,
  coarsely crushed
1 tablespoon brandy
50g (2oz) whole mixed candied peel,
  coarsely chopped
1 egg yolk

1 Soak the raisins in warm water to cover for about 15 minutes until plump, then drain and set aside.

2 Break the chocolate into pieces and place in a large heatproof bowl with the butter. Place over a saucepan of gently simmering water until melted. Remove the bowl from the pan and stir until smooth.

3 Add the sugar, almonds, biscuits, raisins, brandy and candied peel to the melted chocolate and mix well. Return the bowl to the pan and stir in the egg yolk until evenly incorporated. Take off the heat and let the mixture cool completely.

4 Turn the mixture on to a sheet of baking parchment and shape into a roll with your hands. Wrap the 'chocolate salami' in the paper and twist the ends to seal. Refrigerate for several hours to firm up. To serve, remove the paper, cut the salami into thin slices and arrange on a serving plate.

almond biscuits

Almonds are used as a basis for these crisp biscuits from Prato in Tuscany, which are traditionally served with Vin Santo. Their Italian name, *biscotti*, comes from the French '*bis cuit*' meaning 'twice baked'. You can vary the recipe if you like, adding hazelnuts instead of the almonds, or some chopped chocolate.

SERVES 4–6

275g (9oz) Italian '00' flour
175g (6oz) caster sugar
1½ teaspoons baking powder
½ teaspoon salt
2 eggs, plus 1 egg yolk
125g (4oz) blanched whole almonds,
  roughly chopped

1 Preheat the oven to 180°C (fan oven 160°C) gas mark 4. Mix the flour, sugar, baking powder and salt together in a bowl. Add the eggs and egg yolk, and mix well to form a smooth dough. Knead in the chopped almonds.

2 Divide the dough into 4 portions and form each into a cigar-shaped log. Place the logs on a floured baking sheet, spacing them well apart. Bake for about 20 minutes, until golden brown.

3 Cut the logs into 1cm (½ inch) slices while still warm. Separate them and lay on the baking sheet. Bake for another 15 minutes.

4 Transfer the biscuits to a wire rack to cool. Store in an airtight container until required.

index

Acknowledgements

Firstly, I dedicate this book to Mark Salter, who loved life and food in equal measures. Secondly, I should like to thank all those who have helped to make this such a special book: Jane O'Shea for her guidance, Janet Illsley, for her total professionalism, Peter Cassidy for his truly outstanding photography, Linda Tubby for making the food look so wonderful, and Vanessa Courtier for art direction and design. I am also very grateful to Susan Fleming for working with me again and putting me in order, and to Katie O'Donnell for her speed and patience. You are all such fun to work with. Last, but not least, I thank Richard Moore, my husband, for his terrific advice and support.